Break Free

Scripture Decrees to Destroy Strongholds and Walk in Freedom

Mitchell Beecher

Unless otherwise stated, scripture quotations are taken from the World English Bible (WEB), a public domain translation.

ISBN: 979-8-9910968-3-6 (Paperback)
ISBN:979-8-9910968-4-3 (eBook)

Library of Congress Control Number: 2026904533

Book design by Lou Designs.

First printing edition 2026.

www.bekingdombuilders.com

Table of Contents

PREFACE

I wrote this book because I've watched too many believers live beneath what Jesus paid for.

Not because they don't love God. Not because they don't believe the Bible. But because they've learned to tolerate things that are slowly draining their life. They keep showing up, they keep trying, they keep "doing the Christian thing," but behind the scenes they're fighting the same cycles. The same mental pressure. The same private compromises. The same drifting patterns that keep their spiritual life dull and their obedience inconsistent.

And after a while, people stop calling it a battle. They start calling it normal.

That's what burdened me. Because bondage doesn't have to be loud to be deadly. Some strongholds don't show up as obvious addictions. They show up as low-grade fear you can't shake. Apathy you can't explain. Anger you keep excusing. Procrastination you keep spiritualizing. Lust you keep hiding. Offense you keep feeding. And over time, it doesn't just affect you. It affects your marriage. Your family. Your calling. Your confidence. Your ability to build anything that lasts.

This book is my attempt to put something practical in your hands.

Not a book that gives you a moment of inspiration and sends you back into the same routine. Not something written to entertain you. A tool you can return to. Something you can underline, mark up, and use when the fight is real. Something that helps you speak truth when your feelings are loud. Something that pushes you toward repentance when compromise is convenient. Something that calls you into obedience when you've been drifting.

I'm not claiming this book replaces the Bible. It doesn't. Scripture is the authority. It also doesn't replace your local church. You need the body of Christ. What this book is meant to do is help you stop coexisting with what God wants to break, and start moving again with clarity and conviction.

As you read, my encouragement is simple: be honest. Don't read this like a spectator. Don't pick chapters based on what sounds comfortable. Go straight to what's been holding you. Bring it into the light. Agree with God. Obey quickly. And if you have to revisit chapters more than once, do it.

Strongholds don't always collapse in a day, but they do collapse when truth becomes your agreement and obedience becomes your pattern.

My prayer is that this book would help you reclaim ground the enemy has been stealing. That it would rebuild your spiritual backbone. That it would restore your hunger for God. That it would reignite your discipline. And that it would remind you what you were saved for.

You were not saved to spectate.

You were saved to build.

For His glory,
Mitchell Beecher

INTRODUCTION

Some of you have been saved for a long time… but you still feel stuck.

Not "unsure if God is real" stuck. Not "I'm done with church" stuck. I'm talking about the kind of stuck that messes with you because you *do* love Jesus. You *do* believe the Bible. You *do* want to live right. But even with all of that, there are areas in your life that still feel bound. Like you're trying to walk forward while something is quietly pulling you backward.

You know what it's like to have real faith, yet still wrestle with anxiety that won't lift. You know what it's like to have truth in your head, but heaviness in your chest. You know what it's like to want to change, and still find yourself repeating the same patterns. You've prayed. You've promised. You've tried to "do better." And still… the cycle keeps coming back.

If that's you, I need you to hear this from the beginning: you're not crazy, you're not alone, and you're not disqualified. But there may be strongholds in your life that you've learned to manage instead of destroy.

And that's exactly what this book is for.

Because there is a difference between being saved and living free. Salvation is real. The cross is finished. The resurrection is power. But too many believers are living beneath what Jesus paid for. Not because the gospel failed, but because compromise stayed hidden, wounds stayed untouched, and obedience kept getting postponed. The enemy doesn't need you to deny Christ to weaken your life. He just needs you delayed, distracted, passive, and stuck in repeat mode.

This book exists to end that.

Not with hype. Not with spiritual performance. Not with temporary emotion. I'm talking about lasting freedom that shows up in your daily life: your thoughts, your habits, your discipline, your marriage, your money, your purpose, your courage, and your obedience. The kind of freedom where you finally feel clear again. Strong again. Awake again. The kind of freedom where your "yes" to God isn't theoretical. It's practiced.

Because you can't build the Kingdom while you're still chained to what Christ already conquered.

A lot of believers don't realize what's actually happening to them. They assume they just need more motivation. They assume they need a better routine, a stronger personality, or more willpower. They think the problem is that they're "not trying hard enough." But the truth is deeper than that.

Most believers don't need more information. They need transformation.

You can sit under preaching for years and still be bound. You can learn theology and still be trapped in cycles. You can memorize Scripture and still live with constant fear. Knowledge is not the same as freedom. Information is not the same as obedience. And the enemy doesn't mind you being informed. He just doesn't want you walking it out.

Because obedience carries authority.

Obedience produces momentum. Obedience sharpens discernment. Obedience strengthens confidence. Obedience protects marriages. Obedience keeps your mind clean. Obedience shuts doors that the enemy has been using for years. The reason the enemy fights obedience so hard is because once you start obeying God, you stop being easy to push around.

And this is where passive Christianity has wrecked a generation.

A lot of modern Christianity has trained believers to be spectators. To consume sermons like entertainment. To treat spiritual growth like something that happens to them without effort. To call comfort "peace." To call delay "wisdom." To call compromise "struggle." And to call spiritual apathy "burnout."

But you were not saved to spectate.

You were saved to follow Jesus. You were saved to grow. You were saved to be formed into maturity. You were saved to live surrendered. You were saved to carry authority through the Holy Spirit. You were saved to build something with your life that honors God.

The Kingdom of God does not advance through people who agree with truth but never act on it.

And if you're holding this book, I'm going to assume you're done pretending. Done coasting. Done being half-engaged. Done living like your faith is something you "believe," but not something you *obey*.

Because the hard truth is this: you can't pray for breakthrough while you keep feeding what keeps you bound.

Some believers want power without purity. They want clarity without commitment. They want peace without surrender. They want authority while still keeping secret agreements with fear, lust, anger, offense, or addiction. They want God to move, but they won't close the door. They keep asking the Lord to remove what He already told them to crucify.

That's not condemnation. That's conviction, and conviction is mercy.

Conviction is God loving you enough to confront the chain instead of letting you live with it.

So why did I build this book around declarations and decrees?

Because whether you realize it or not, you are already declaring things every day. Your mouth is not neutral. The words you speak are not harmless. They shape your agreement, your expectation, your identity, and the direction of your life.

When you say, "I'll never change," you are declaring something.
When you say, "This is just how I am," you are declaring something.
When you say, "I can't stop," you are declaring something.
When you say, "Nothing works for me," you are declaring something.
When you say, "I'm always going to struggle," you are declaring something.

You may not call it a decree, but it's a decree. It's agreement.

And if you keep agreeing with bondage, you will keep living under bondage.

This book trains you to change your agreement. Not with hype, not with emotional manipulation, and not with fake confidence. It trains you to come into alignment with what God has already said. It teaches you to speak truth when your feelings are loud. It teaches you to answer lies with Scripture. It teaches you to confront darkness instead of negotiating with it.

Jesus didn't defeat temptation by ignoring it. He didn't defeat the devil by staying silent. He didn't "think positive" His way into victory. He answered with the Word of God.

"It is written."

That's not just a moment in the wilderness. That's a blueprint for warfare.

Because the enemy loves believers who stay quiet. He loves when you fight everything internally but never open your mouth. He loves when your mind spirals in fear, shame, or fantasy and you just sit there absorbing it like it's normal. He loves when you treat spiritual attacks like they're untouchable realities instead of lies that must be confronted.

But when a believer starts speaking truth and backing it with obedience, something shifts.

Not because the believer is powerful in themselves, but because God's Word is alive, and truth breaks agreements that lies were feeding.

Now here's the part that matters most: freedom is not the finish line.

Freedom is the starting line.

God does not set you free just so you can finally "feel better." He sets you free so you can finally *live right.* So you can love your spouse correctly. So you can lead your home with strength. So you can wake up with clarity. So you can serve with consistency. So you can stop being a consumer and become a builder. So you can stop being tossed around by temptation and start walking like a man or woman who is actually submitted to Jesus.

You are not just being rescued from something in this book.

You are being released for something.

This is where so many believers miss it. They treat freedom like an emotional event instead of a spiritual path. They want the outcome without the obedience. They want deliverance without discipline. They want the chains to break, but they don't want to change the habits that keep rebuilding the cage.

But real freedom always produces fruit.

True faith produces obedience. The gospel is not just forgiveness. It is transformation. Jesus is not just Savior. He is Lord. That means freedom is not simply about what God removes. It's also about what I choose to obey once He does.

And yes, some of the battles addressed in this book are deeply personal. Some are hidden. Some are private. Some are shameful. Some are things people don't talk about in church because they're afraid of being exposed. But hiding doesn't heal you. Secrecy doesn't protect you. Darkness doesn't get weaker when you ignore it.

It gets stronger.

And we need to talk about something else that modern Christianity often avoids: spiritual warfare.

Not everything is demonic. Not every struggle is a devil. Not every hard season means you're oppressed. Sometimes you're just undisciplined. Sometimes you're wounded. Sometimes you're in sin and you need to repent. Sometimes you're tired and you need rest. We don't blame demons for everything.

But we also don't pretend the devil isn't real.

Because the Bible is clear: "Our struggle is not against flesh and blood" (Ephesians 6:12). That means some resistance is spiritual. Some torment is not just emotional. Some pressure is not just stress. Some battles are attacks designed to wear you down, dull your appetite for God, and keep you passive. And if you treat a spiritual battle like it's only psychological, you will stay stuck trying to win with the wrong weapons.

That's why this book doesn't just comfort you. It arms you.

It gives you language for repentance. It gives you Scripture for warfare. It gives you declarations to draw a line in the sand. It gives you decrees to replace lies with truth. It gives you obedience steps so you don't walk away inspired but unchanged.

Because freedom isn't maintained by feelings.

Freedom is maintained by obedience.

So here's how I want you to approach this book.

Don't skim it. Don't rush it. Don't read it like content. Read it like a weapon. Read it like you're done playing games. Read it like you're ready to build.

And let me make this clear from the start: **this book is not designed to be read straight through like a normal book.** You *can* read it cover to cover, but that's not the main purpose. This is a battlefield manual. A toolbox. A set of spiritual weapons. That means you don't start at chapter one just because it's chapter one. You start where the fight is hottest in your life right now.

Each chapter is built with structure on purpose because strongholds don't break through randomness. They break through clear truth, repeated alignment, and practiced obedience. Some chapters may feel intense. Good. Strongholds don't respond to soft Christianity. They respond to surrender, truth, and spiritual authority in Christ.

So don't start where it's comfortable. Start where you're most bound. Don't avoid the chapter that exposes you. Don't skip the one that touches your secret life. Don't pretend you're fine if you know you're not. Go straight for the chain that keeps yanking you back, and deal with it in the light. Close the doors. Speak the truth. Obey the instruction. And keep going until the pattern breaks.

You're not trying to impress God by reading a book.
You're responding to the mercy of God who refuses to leave you stuck.

So let me say it plainly: you were not saved to spectate. You were saved to build. And the pages ahead are not just here to help you break free from something… they are here to help you break free **for** something.

Now open to the chapter that hits you.
And let's get you free.

CHAPTER 1

Break Free From Anxiety & Fear
You weren't created to live on edge.

OPENING PRAYER

Father, in Jesus' name, I come to You right now and I refuse to live ruled by fear. I repent for trusting my anxious thoughts more than Your Word. Holy Spirit, strengthen me, steady my mind, and teach me to walk in obedience and peace. Amen.

THE ISSUE

Anxiety and fear don't always look like panic. Sometimes it looks like overthinking, worst-case scenarios, irritability, shutting down, constant tension, and living one bad headline away from spiraling.

It's your body bracing for impact that never comes… and your mind rehearsing pain that hasn't happened yet. And over time, fear doesn't just *visit* - it starts *leading*.

WHY IT'S HAPPENING

- You've been trying to control what only God can carry.
- Your mind has been trained to scan for danger instead of anchored in truth.
- You keep feeding the fear pipeline (news, doom scrolling, "what if" loops, isolation).
- You're carrying pressure without casting it on the Lord.
- You've been treating fear like a personality trait instead of an enemy to resist.

WHERE IT CAME FROM

For many believers, fear began as protection: after a loss, betrayal, trauma, disappointment, or repeated stress. But what started as caution became a mindset… and then it became a habit.

The door stayed open through constant mental rehearsal, isolation, and trying to manage life without spiritual dependence. And the lie underneath it usually sounds like this: "If I don't stay worried, something bad will happen, and God won't come through." That lie is loud, but it's still a lie.

BREAK FREE DECLARATION

I break agreement with anxiety and fear in the name of Jesus Christ.
I reject the lie that I am unsafe, alone, and powerless.
Jesus is Lord over my mind, my body, my thoughts, and my future.
I will not be led by panic. I will be led by truth.
I choose obedience, prayer, and trust, and I receive the peace God promised me.

SCRIPTURE-BACKED DECREES

1. Fear will not lead me. I declare that fear is not my portion, according to 2 Timothy 1:7, which says, *"For God didn't give us a spirit of fear, but of power, love, and self-control."*

2. His presence steadies me. I decree that God is with me and I am not alone, as it is written in Isaiah 41:10, *"Don't you be afraid, for I am with you… I will strengthen you… I will help you."*

3. My worry becomes worship. I declare that my mind will not spiral. My mind will pray, in alignment with Philippians 4:6, *"In nothing be anxious… by prayer… let your requests be made known to God."*

4. Peace is my protection. I decree that God's peace guards me when I obey His Word, based on Philippians 4:7, *"The peace of God… will guard your hearts and your thoughts in Christ Jesus."*

5. I am cared for. I declare that I cast my burdens on the Lord today because Scripture declares in 1 Peter 5:7, *"casting all your worries on him because he cares for you."*

6. I receive His peace. I decree that my heart will not be troubled or

fearful, in accordance with John 14:27, *"Don't let your heart be troubled, neither let it be fearful."*

7.   I live today in faith. I declare that I will not borrow tomorrow's trouble, according to Matthew 6:34, *"Therefore don't be anxious for tomorrow… Each day's own evil is sufficient."*

8.   My mind is staying on Christ. I decree that God keeps my mind in peace when I stay fixed on Him, as God says in Isaiah 26:3, *"You will keep whoever's mind is steadfast in perfect peace because he trusts in you."*

9.   I trust God completely. I declare that my trust is in the Lord, not in my own understanding, in agreement with Proverbs 3:5, *"Trust in Yahweh with all your heart, and don't lean on your own understanding."*

10. He is guiding me. I decree that God directs my path as I acknowledge Him, according to Proverbs 3:6, *"In all your ways acknowledge him, and he will make your paths straight."*

11. Fear is losing ground. I declare that the Lord is my light and my salvation, as it is written in Psalm 27:1, *"Yahweh is my light and my salvation. Whom shall I fear?"*

12. My reflex is trust. I decree that I will remember God in the moment fear rises, based on Psalm 56:3, *"When I am afraid, I will put my trust in you."*

13. Help is present, not distant. I declare that the Lord is my refuge right now, according to Psalm 46:1, *"God is our refuge and strength, a very present help in trouble."*

14. God is not leaving. I decree that I will not be abandoned because Scripture declares in Hebrews 13:5, *"I will in no way leave you, neither will I in any way forsake you."*

15. I am helped. I declare that I can face what comes with courage, as it is written in Hebrews 13:6, *"The Lord is my helper. I will not fear."*

16. I decree that I will not be ruled by sudden dread, based on Proverbs

3:25, *"Don't be afraid of sudden fear, neither of the desolation of the wicked when it comes."*
My heart stays steady.

17. I declare that the Lord delivers me from fear as I seek Him, according to Psalm 34:4, *"I sought Yahweh, and he answered me, and delivered me from all my fears."*
Deliverance is real.

18. God is with me in the valley. I decree that even in dark seasons, I will not fear because Scripture declares in Psalm 23:4, *"Even though I walk through the valley of the shadow of death, I will fear no evil; for you are with me."*

19. I respond with wisdom. I declare that God gives me wisdom instead of panic, in agreement with James 1:5, *"But if any of you lacks wisdom, let him ask of God... and it will be given."*

20. My mind will submit. I decree that I take every thought captive in obedience to Christ, according to 2 Corinthians 10:5, *"bringing every thought into captivity to the obedience of Christ."*

21. Bad news won't own me. I declare that God is my shield and I will not be afraid of bad news, in accordance with Psalm 112:7, *"He will not be afraid of evil news. His heart is steadfast, trusting in Yahweh."*

22. God is my refuge. I decree that I will dwell in God's shelter and speak trust out loud, based on Psalm 91:1–2, *"He who dwells in the secret place... will say of Yahweh, 'He is my refuge and my fortress.'"*

23. Courage is my standard. I declare that the Lord will strengthen me when I obey Him, according to Joshua 1:9, *"Be strong and courageous... for Yahweh your God is with you wherever you go."*

OBEDIENCE ACTIVATION

Confession

Jesus, I repent for partnering with anxiety and fear, and I surrender my mind
to You.

Action Steps

- Pray first, not last. The moment anxiety rises, pray out loud for 60
  seconds.
- Replace the input. Cut off fear-feeding content (doom scrolling,
  panic talk, obsessive checking).
- Take the thought captive. Label the lie and replace it with a verse
  from this chapter.
- Move your body in obedience. Walk, breathe, and worship. Don't
  sit and spiral.
- Bring it into the light. Talk to a mature believer or pastor instead of
  suffering in silence.

Accountability Move

Today, I will text one trusted believer: "I'm breaking agreement with
anxiety. Pray with me."

CLOSING PRAYER

Father, in Jesus' name, I bring You my fears, my stress, and my constant
"what ifs." I repent for living like I'm alone, and I choose to trust You as my
refuge and my Father. I renounce every lie that tells me I'm unsafe,
powerless, or forgotten. Holy Spirit, fill me with power, love, and self-
control, and train my mind to stay on truth. I receive Your peace, I submit to
Your Word, and I will walk in obedience today. In the name of Jesus, amen.

CHAPTER 2

Break Free From Depression & Hopelessness

Break free from the fog that convinces you nothing will change.

OPENING PRAYER

Father, in Jesus' name, I come to You and I refuse to surrender to darkness. I repent for agreeing with hopeless thoughts, and I ask You to restore strength to my soul. Holy Spirit, breathe life into me again and lead me into truth, step by step. Amen.

THE ISSUE

Depression isn't always tears on the floor. Sometimes it's numbness, exhaustion, emptiness, irritability, and the quiet belief that nothing matters.

It's waking up with no desire, no energy, and no expectation. Just survival. And hopelessness is the most dangerous part because it convinces you this is permanent.

WHY IT'S HAPPENING

- You've been carrying pain without releasing it to God.
- Your mind has been repeating loss instead of rehearsing truth.
- Isolation has amplified the darkness.
- Disappointment has become a lens instead of a season.
- You've started believing feelings are facts.

WHERE IT CAME FROM

For many people, depression starts after something breaks: grief, rejection, failure, betrayal, chronic stress, or seasons where prayers felt unanswered.

The root is pain, but the door stays open through isolation, unresolved grief, and constant agreement with thoughts that drain life. It becomes a cycle: low energy leads to withdrawal, withdrawal strengthens darkness, and darkness steals desire.

And the lie underneath it usually sounds like this: "Nothing will ever change, and God is not coming." That lie is not wisdom. It's oppression.

BREAK FREE DECLARATION

I break agreement with depression and hopelessness in the name of Jesus Christ.
I reject the lie that my life is over, my joy is gone, and my future is closed.
Jesus is Lord over my mind, my emotions, and my inner world.
I will not be led by despair. I will be led by truth.
I receive the joy of the Lord, and I choose obedience even when my feelings resist.

SCRIPTURE-BACKED DECREES

1. God is near to me. I declare that I am not abandoned in this battle, according to Psalm 34:18, *"Yahweh is near to those who have a broken heart, and saves those who have a crushed spirit."*

2. Heaviness must lift. I decree that my soul will not stay trapped in heaviness, as it is written in Isaiah 61:3, *"the oil of joy instead of mourning, the garment of praise instead of a spirit of heaviness."*

3. Strength is returning. I declare that the joy of the Lord strengthens me, based on Nehemiah 8:10, *"for the joy of Yahweh is your strength."*

4. I will not collapse. I decree that God renews my strength when I hope in Him, according to Isaiah 40:31, *"those who wait for Yahweh will renew their strength."*

5. Today holds mercy. I declare that God's mercies are new for me today, just as the Word says in Lamentations 3:22–23, *"His compassions fail not. They are new every morning."*

6. My hope has a source. I decree that I will not be consumed by despair, in agreement with Lamentations 3:24, *"Yahweh is my portion… therefore I will hope in him."*

7. My pain is not ignored. I declare that my tears are seen and counted by God, according to Psalm 56:8, *"You count my wanderings. You put my tears into your container."*

8. Comfort is available. I decree that I will be comforted by God Himself, based on 2 Corinthians 1:3–4, *"the Father of mercies and God of all comfort... comforts us in all our affliction."*

9. Hope will fill me again. I declare that I will not surrender to hopeless thinking, according to Romans 15:13, *"may the God of hope fill you with all joy and peace in believing."*

10. God is working in me. I decree that I have purpose even in dark seasons, as it is written in Romans 8:28, *"all things work together for good for those who love God."*

11. Help is present. I declare that God is my refuge and strength in this moment, according to Psalm 46:1, *"God is our refuge and strength, a very present help in trouble."*

12. My soul will rise. I decree that I will not stay bowed down in my soul because Scripture declares in Psalm 42:11, *"Why are you in despair, my soul?... Hope in God!"*

13. Restoration is happening. I declare that God restores my soul, based on Psalm 23:3, *"He restores my soul."*

14. Ashes are not my ending. I decree that God gives beauty for ashes, in alignment with Isaiah 61:3, *"to give to them beauty for ashes."*

15. Joy is still coming. I declare that I will rejoice again, as God promises in Psalm 30:5, *"Weeping may stay for the night, but joy comes in the morning."*

16. I am not alone. I decree that I will not fear the valley because God is with me, according to Psalm 23:4, *"I will fear no evil, for you are with me."*

17. My head will lift. I declare that God is able to lift my head, according to Psalm 3:3, *"you, Yahweh, are a shield... and the one*

who lifts up my head."

18. My thoughts will be protected. I decree that my mind will be guarded by God's peace, based on Philippians 4:7, *"The peace of God... will guard your hearts and your thoughts in Christ Jesus."*

19. Praise breaks darkness. I declare that I will praise even when I don't feel it, as it is written in Psalm 34:1, *"His praise will always be in my mouth."*

20. Strength is not gone. I decree that God gives me strength when I feel weak, according to Isaiah 41:10, *"I will strengthen you. Yes, I will help you."*

21. My emptiness will be filled. I declare that the Lord satisfies my soul with good, based on Psalm 107:9, *"For he satisfies the longing soul."*

22. Light is breaking in. I decree that my life will not end in darkness, as it is written in Micah 7:8, *"When I fall, I will arise. When I sit in darkness, Yahweh will be a light to me."*

23. I will move forward. I declare that I can do the next obedient step through Christ, according to Philippians 4:13, *"I can do all things through Christ, who strengthens me."*

24. I will live. I decree that I will not die spiritually in this season because Scripture declares in Psalm 118:17, *"I will not die, but live, and declare Yah's works."*

OBEDIENCE ACTIVATION

Confession

Jesus, I repent for agreeing with hopelessness, and I surrender my mind and emotions to You.

Action Steps

- Speak one decree out loud every morning before you check your phone.

- Move your body daily (walk, sunlight, breathing, simple discipline) even when you feel numb.
- Break isolation on purpose by calling or meeting with one trusted believer this week.
- Replace the soundtrack by cutting off depressing content and filling your atmosphere with worship and Scripture.
- Serve someone small. One act of obedience to break self-focused fog.

Accountability Move

Today, I will message one trusted person: "I've been battling heaviness. Can you pray with me and check on me?"

CLOSING PRAYER

Father, in Jesus' name, I bring You my heaviness, my numbness, and the thoughts that tell me nothing will change. I repent for agreeing with despair and for letting darkness shape my expectations. I receive Your comfort, Your strength, and the hope You promised in Your Word. Holy Spirit, lift the fog, renew my mind, and give me grace for the next obedient step. I declare that joy will return, strength will rise, and I will not stay here. In the name of Jesus, amen.

CHAPTER 3

Break Free From Shame & Condemnation

Conviction leads to repentance. Condemnation leads to hiding.

OPENING PRAYER

Father, in Jesus' name, I come out of hiding and I come into Your light. I repent for agreeing with shame and condemning myself when You have offered forgiveness. Holy Spirit, cleanse my conscience, renew my mind, and teach me to walk in freedom. Amen.

THE ISSUE

Shame isn't just guilt over what I did. It's the belief that what you did is who your are. Condemnation is the voice that says, "You're disqualified. You'll never change. God is done with you."

It doesn't lead me to repentance. It leads you to hiding, isolation, and spiritual silence. And the enemy loves shame because a believer in shame won't pray with confidence.

WHY IT'S HAPPENING

- You keep rehearsing your failure instead of receiving God's forgiveness.
- You confuse conviction with condemnation and call both "God."
- You haven't fully brought what happened into the light.
- You've let your past become your identity.
- You're trying to punish yourself for what Jesus already paid for.

WHERE IT CAME FROM

Shame often began after a fall, a secret, a compromise, or a moment that changed the way you saw yourself. Sometimes it started in childhood through rejection, ridicule, or constant criticism, where you learned to feel "not enough."

The door stays open through secrecy, self-hatred, and refusing to believe that God actually cleanses. And the lie underneath it sounds like this: "God forgives other people, but I'm too dirty to be free." That lie is not humility. It's unbelief.

BREAK FREE DECLARATION

I break agreement with shame and condemnation in the name of Jesus Christ.
I reject the lie that my past is my identity and my failure is my future.
Jesus is Lord over my story, my mind, and my conscience.
I receive forgiveness, cleansing, and restoration through the blood of Jesus.
I will live in the light, walk in obedience, and speak with confidence again.

SCRIPTURE-BACKED DECREES

1. Condemnation is not my covering. I declare that there is no condemnation for me in Christ Jesus, according to Romans 8:1, "There is therefore now no condemnation to those who are in Christ Jesus."

2. My forgiveness is real. I decree that God is faithful to forgive and cleanse me when I confess, as it is written in 1 John 1:9, "If we confess our sins, he is faithful and righteous to forgive us the sins, and to cleanse us from all unrighteousness."

3. My conscience will be cleaned. I declare that the blood of Jesus purifies my conscience, based on Hebrews 9:14, "the blood of Christ… will cleanse your conscience from dead works to serve the living God."

4. My sin is not stronger than grace. I decree that where sin increased, grace abounded more, according to Romans 5:20, "But where sin increased, grace abounded more exceedingly."

5. God does not despise a broken heart. I decree that He receives me when I repent sincerely, as the Word says in Psalm 51:17, "a broken and contrite heart, O God, you will not despise."

6. My past is not my label. I declare that I am a new creation in Christ,

according to 2 Corinthians 5:17, "Therefore if anyone is in Christ, he is a new creation. The old things have passed away."

7. God's mercy is not running out. I decree that His compassions are new every morning, according to Lamentations 3:22–23, "His compassions fail not. They are new every morning."

8. Jesus is not holding my sin over my head. I declare that He forgives completely, based on Psalm 103:12, "As far as the east is from the west, so far has he removed our transgressions from us."

9. I am not rejected. I decree that I am accepted in Christ and brought near to God, according to Ephesians 1:6, "to the praise of the glory of his grace, by which he freely gave us favor in the Beloved."

10. My accusations are answered by the cross. I declare that God justifies me, according to Romans 8:33, "Who could bring a charge against God's chosen ones? It is God who justifies."

11. The enemy's voice is not final. I decree that the accuser is overcome by the blood of the Lamb, as it is written in Revelation 12:10–11, "the accuser… has been thrown down… They overcame him because of the Lamb's blood."

12. My weakness does not disqualify me. I declare that God's grace is sufficient for me, according to 2 Corinthians 12:9, "My grace is sufficient for you, for my power is made perfect in weakness."

13. I will run to God, not away from Him. I decree that I can approach the throne of grace with confidence, based on Hebrews 4:16, "Let us therefore draw near with boldness to the throne of grace."

14. God restores what sin tried to destroy. I declare that He is able to redeem and restore, according to Joel 2:25, "I will restore to you the years that the swarming locust has eaten."

15. I will live in the light. I decree that walking in the light brings cleansing, according to 1 John 1:7, "if we walk in the light… the blood of Jesus Christ… cleanses us from all sin."

16. God does not break bruised people. I declare that Jesus deals gently

with the weak, as it is written in Isaiah 42:3, "He won't break a
bruised reed. He won't quench a dimly burning wick."

17. My identity is anchored in God's love. I decree that nothing can
    separate me from His love, according to Romans 8:38–39,
    "nothing… will be able to separate us from the love of God."

18. I am not filthy in God's eyes. I declare that He washes and makes
    me clean, based on Isaiah 1:18, "Though your sins be as scarlet,
    they shall be as white as snow."

19. Repentance is the path forward, not punishment. I decree that godly
    sorrow produces repentance leading to salvation, according to 2
    Corinthians 7:10, "godly sorrow produces repentance leading to
    salvation… but the sorrow of the world produces death."

20. The Lord strengthens me when I return to Him. I declare that He
    upholds me with His hand, according to Isaiah 41:10, "I will
    strengthen you. Yes, I will help you. Yes, I will uphold you with the
    right hand of my righteousness."

21. I will not be stuck in yesterday. I decree that I forget what is behind
    and press forward, according to Philippians 3:13–14, "forgetting the
    things which are behind… I press on toward the goal."

22. God finishes what He starts in me. I declare that He will complete
    His work, according to Philippians 1:6, "he who began a good work
    in you will complete it."

23. My life will produce fruit again. I decree that Jesus restores and re-
    anchors me in purpose, based on John 15:5, "He who remains in
    me… the same bears much fruit."

OBEDIENCE ACTIVATION

Confession

Jesus, I repent for agreeing with shame and condemnation, and I receive
Your forgiveness and cleansing.

Action Steps

- Confess fully and specifically to God instead of vague prayers and hidden guilt.
- Bring it into the light with a mature believer, pastor, or trusted accountability partner.
- Replace the shame script by speaking 3 decrees out loud every day for 7 days.
- Remove the trigger environment that keeps pulling you back into compromise.
- Obey immediately when conviction comes. No delays. No negotiating.

Accountability Move

Today, I will tell one trusted believer, "I'm breaking shame off my life. Please pray and hold me accountable."

CLOSING PRAYER

Father, in Jesus' name, I repent for hiding, self-hatred, and living under condemnation when You offered me cleansing. I receive the forgiveness of Jesus Christ and the freedom of a clean conscience. Holy Spirit, renew my mind, strengthen my heart, and train me to walk in the light with confidence and obedience. I break agreement with shame, I reject every lie of disqualification, and I choose truth. Thank You that my past is not my identity and my future is not canceled. In the name of Jesus, amen.

CHAPTER 4

Break Free From Comparison & Envy

The quickest way to hate your life is to stare at somebody else's.

OPENING PRAYER

Father, in Jesus' name, I repent for comparing my life to others and letting envy poison my heart. I renounce the lie that I am behind, forgotten, or less than. Holy Spirit, reset my focus, purify my desires, and teach me contentment with obedience. Amen.

THE ISSUE

Comparison is a thief that never stops taking. It steals joy, peace, gratitude, confidence, and purpose, and leaves me restless and bitter.

Envy is the quiet resentment that rises when someone else gets what you wanted or becomes what you hoped to be. And if you don't break it, you will end up hating your life while God is trying to grow you in it.

WHY IT'S HAPPENING

- You're measuring your life by someone else's highlight reel.
- You're craving recognition instead of valuing obedience.
- You're impatient with your process and suspicious of God's timing.
- You're scrolling too much and thanking God too little.
- You've confused "different assignment" with "unfair treatment."

WHERE IT CAME FROM

Comparison often started when you learned to evaluate yourself by outcomes, applause, attention, money, looks, titles, or "progress." The root is insecurity, but the door stays open through constant exposure, constant measuring, and constant dissatisfaction.

Instead of focusing on what God told you to build, you keep staring

sideways at someone else's lane. And the lie underneath it sounds like this:
"God is blessing them more than me because I'm less valuable." That lie is
not truth. It's a trap.

BREAK FREE DECLARATION

I break agreement with comparison, envy, and jealousy in the name of Jesus
Christ.
I reject the lie that I am behind, overlooked, or forgotten by God.
Jesus is Lord over my identity, my timeline, and my assignment.
I will not resent another person's blessing. I will honor God's process in my
life.
I choose gratitude, contentment, and obedience, and I receive peace in my
calling.

SCRIPTURE-BACKED DECREES

1. I will not envy what God has given another person. I declare that
   envy leads to confusion and evil, according to James 3:16, "For
   where jealousy and selfish ambition are, there is confusion and
   every evil deed."

2. My value is not measured by what others have. I decree that I am
   created in the image of God, according to Genesis 1:27, "God
   created man in his own image… male and female he created them."

3. God's plan for my life is not behind schedule. I declare that God
   makes everything beautiful in its time, according to Ecclesiastes
   3:11, "He has made everything beautiful in its time."

4. Contentment is possible because God is faithful. I decree that
   Godliness with contentment is great gain, according to 1 Timothy
   6:6, "But godliness with contentment is great gain."

5. I will not be ruled by a craving for more. I declare that I will keep
   my life free from the love of money, according to Hebrews 13:5,
   "Be free from the love of money… be content with such things as
   you have."

6. God will not abandon me in my season. I decree that He will never

leave or forsake me, according to Hebrews 13:5, "I will in no way leave you, neither will I in any way forsake you."

7. I am not called to compete with my brother. I declare that I will not compare myself with others, according to Galatians 6:4, "But let each man test his own work… not in comparison with his neighbor."

8. My responsibility is obedience, not scoreboard watching. I decree that each person carries their own load, according to Galatians 6:5, "For each man will bear his own burden."

9. I will rejoice with others instead of resenting them. I declare that I will celebrate God's work in others, according to Romans 12:15, "Rejoice with those who rejoice."

10. My heart will not rot with jealousy. I decree that envy is rottenness to the bones, according to Proverbs 14:30, "A sound heart is the life of the flesh; but envy is the rottenness of the bones."

11. God's blessing in someone else's life is not my threat. I declare that every good gift comes from God, according to James 1:17, "Every good gift and every perfect gift is from above."

12. I will not despise small beginnings. I decree that God honors growth and process, according to Zechariah 4:10, "For who despises the day of small things?"

13. I will not trade peace for applause. I declare that seeking man's approval is a trap, according to Proverbs 29:25, "The fear of man proves to be a snare."

14. I will keep my eyes on what God assigned me. I decree that I run my race with endurance, according to Hebrews 12:1, "let us run with perseverance the race that is set before us."

15. Jesus is the focus, not the crowd. I declare that I fix my eyes on Jesus, according to Hebrews 12:2, "looking to Jesus, the author and perfecter of faith."

16. I will not let pride disguise itself as ambition. I decree that I will not

do anything through selfish ambition, according to Philippians 2:3, "doing nothing through rivalry or through conceit."

17. I will honor others without losing myself. I declare that I count others better than myself with humility, according to Philippians 2:3, "in humility, each counting others better than himself."

18. God has prepared good works for my life specifically. I decree that I walk in what He prepared for me, according to Ephesians 2:10, "created in Christ Jesus for good works… that we should walk in them."

19. My assignment is real even if it's quiet. I declare that the Lord establishes the work of my hands, according to Psalm 90:17, "Establish the work of our hands for us."

20. I will not envy the wicked or their success. I decree that I will not be jealous of evildoers, according to Psalm 37:1, "Don't fret because of evildoers, neither be envious against those who work unrighteousness."

21. My peace increases when I trust God's timing. I declare that the Lord gives me peace as I trust Him, according to Isaiah 26:3, "You will keep whoever's mind is steadfast in perfect peace because he trusts in you."

22. I will measure my life by Christ, not by social proof. I decree that my boast is only in the Lord, according to 2 Corinthians 10:17, "But he who boasts, let him boast in the Lord."

23. I will be thankful in every season. I declare that God calls me to gratitude, according to 1 Thessalonians 5:18, "In everything give thanks."

24. I will not let another person's life make me bitter. I decree that love is not jealous, according to 1 Corinthians 13:4, "Love… is not jealous."

OBEDIENCE ACTIVATION

Confession

Jesus, I repent for comparison and envy, and I surrender my desires and my timeline to You.

Action Steps

- Delete or mute what triggers envy (accounts, pages, content that stirs dissatisfaction).
- Turn comparison into prayer by thanking God for someone else's blessing instead of resenting it.
- Write down what God told you to build and take one obedient step today.
- Practice daily gratitude by listing 5 gifts God has already given you.
- Serve someone to break the inward spiral of self-focus.

Accountability Move

Today, I will tell one trusted believer, "I'm battling comparison. Help me stay focused on my lane."

CLOSING PRAYER

Father, in Jesus' name, I repent for comparing my life to others and letting envy distort my heart. I renounce jealousy, resentment, and every lie that tells me I'm behind or forgotten. Holy Spirit, cleanse my desires, strengthen my gratitude, and anchor me in obedience to my assignment. Teach me to honor what You're doing in others without despising what You're doing in me. I receive contentment, peace, and confidence in Your timing and Your calling. In the name of Jesus, amen.

CHAPTER 5

Break Free From Double-Mindedness

One foot in. One foot out. No stability. No authority.

OPENING PRAYER

Father, in Jesus' name, I repent for being divided, inconsistent, and unstable in my walk with You. I renounce compromise, hesitation, and every excuse that keeps me half-committed. Holy Spirit, strengthen my heart, settle my decisions, and lead me into wholehearted obedience. Amen.

THE ISSUE

Double-mindedness is living split. It's wanting God, but also wanting control. Wanting freedom, but still feeding the flesh. Wanting purpose, but staying comfortable.

It's spiritual indecision disguised as "I'm still figuring it out." But the truth is simple: when you're divided, you're unstable, and instability kills authority.

WHY IT'S HAPPENING

- You keep trying to serve two masters without fully surrendering to Jesus.
- You crave comfort more than transformation.
- You're delaying decisions God already made clear.
- You're letting fear of sacrifice keep you in the middle.
- You're feeding both the Spirit and the flesh and wondering why you feel weak.

WHERE IT CAME FROM

Double-mindedness often starts when you want the benefits of following Jesus, but you're afraid of the cost. The root is usually fear: fear of change, fear of losing control, fear of discomfort, fear of what obedience might require.

The door stays open through compromise, repeated delays, secret sin, and constant negotiating with conviction. And the lie underneath it sounds like this: "I can stay in the middle and still be safe." But the middle isn't safety. It's instability.

BREAK FREE DECLARATION

I break agreement with double-mindedness and spiritual compromise in the name of Jesus Christ.
I reject the lie that partial obedience is enough and that indecision is harmless.
Jesus is Lord, and I will not live divided between truth and comfort.
I choose wholehearted surrender, clear decisions, and consistent obedience.
I receive stability, strength, and authority through the Holy Spirit.

SCRIPTURE-BACKED DECREES

1. God is not calling me to be divided. I declare that a double-minded man is unstable in all his ways, according to James 1:8, "He is a double-minded man, unstable in all his ways."

2. Faith requires clear direction. I decree that I will ask God in faith without doubting, according to James 1:6, "But let him ask in faith, nothing doubting."

3. I will not live in hesitation. I declare that doubt makes me tossed around and unstable, according to James 1:6, "For he who doubts is like a wave of the sea, driven by the wind and tossed."

4. Indecision will not rule my life. I decree that I will not waver between two opinions, according to 1 Kings 18:21, "How long will you waver between the two sides? If Yahweh is God, follow him."

5. Jesus is Lord, not a suggestion. I declare that I will serve the Lord fully, according to Joshua 24:15, "Choose this day whom you will serve… but as for me and my house, we will serve Yahweh."

6. I will not try to serve two masters. I decree that I cannot serve God and another ruler, according to Matthew 6:24, "You can't serve God and Mammon."

7. My heart will be made whole. I declare that God searches my heart and leads me in truth, according to Psalm 139:23–24, "Search me, God… lead me in the everlasting way."

8. I will not keep hidden compromise. I decree that whoever conceals sin will not prosper, according to Proverbs 28:13, "Whoever conceals his sins doesn't prosper."

9. Repentance produces stability. I declare that confessing and renouncing sin leads to mercy, according to Proverbs 28:13, "but whoever confesses and renounces them finds mercy."

10. My obedience will not be partial. I decree that I will fear God and keep His commandments, according to Ecclesiastes 12:13, "Fear God, and keep his commandments; for this is the whole duty of man."

11. My mind will be renewed, not negotiated. I declare that I will be transformed by renewal, according to Romans 12:2, "be transformed by the renewing of your mind."

12. I will not be conformed to the world. I decree that I reject the patterns that weaken me, according to Romans 12:2, "Don't be conformed to this world."

13. I belong fully to Jesus. I declare that I was bought with a price, according to 1 Corinthians 6:20, "for you were bought with a price."

14. My body will not lead my spirit. I decree that I present myself to God, according to Romans 6:13, "present yourselves to God, as alive from the dead."

15. Sin will not have dominion over me. I declare that I am under grace with power to obey, according to Romans 6:14, "For sin will not have dominion over you."

16. I will walk by the Spirit, not by impulse. I decree that I will not fulfill the lust of the flesh, according to Galatians 5:16, "Walk by the Spirit, and you won't fulfill the lust of the flesh."

17. I will stop feeding both sides. I declare that the flesh and Spirit are opposed, according to Galatians 5:17, "For the flesh lusts against the Spirit… and the Spirit against the flesh."

18. My choices will match my confession. I decree that I will not merely hear the Word but do it, according to James 1:22, "But be doers of the word, and not only hearers."

19. I am built for endurance, not quitting. I declare that perseverance produces maturity, according to James 1:4, "Let perseverance have its perfect work, that you may be perfect and complete."

20. God strengthens me to stand firm. I decree that I will be strong and courageous in obedience, according to Joshua 1:9, "Be strong and courageous… for Yahweh your God is with you wherever you go."

21. My stability comes from staying close to Christ. I declare that remaining in Jesus produces fruit, according to John 15:5, "He who remains in me… bears much fruit."

22. I will not drift away from truth. I decree that I hold fast my confession without wavering, according to Hebrews 10:23, "Let's hold fast the confession of our hope without wavering."

23. I will submit to God and resist the devil. I declare that resistance begins with surrender, according to James 4:7, "Be subject therefore to God. Resist the devil, and he will flee from you."

24. My decisions will be clear and obedient. I decree that I commit my works to the Lord, according to Proverbs 16:3, "Commit your deeds to Yahweh, and your plans shall succeed."

OBEDIENCE ACTIVATION

Confession

Jesus, I repent for double-mindedness and compromise, and I surrender fully to You as Lord.

Action Steps

- Remove the "middle ground" today by cutting off one compromise that keeps pulling you back.
- Make one clear decision you've been delaying and obey immediately.
- Confess hidden sin to God and bring it into the light with a trusted believer.
- Build consistency by praying daily and speaking 3 decrees out loud for 7 days.
- Stop feeding the flesh by removing one trigger source (content, habit, environment).

Accountability Move

Today, I will tell one trusted believer, "I'm done living divided. Help me stay accountable to obedience."

CLOSING PRAYER

Father, in Jesus' name, I repent for living divided, hesitating in obedience, and negotiating with conviction. I renounce compromise, fear, and every lie that tells me partial surrender is enough. Holy Spirit, strengthen my heart, renew my mind, and make my obedience consistent. I choose wholehearted devotion to Jesus Christ, and I receive stability and authority through Your Word. Seal this decision in me, and teach me to stand firm without wavering. In the name of Jesus, amen.

CHAPTER 6

Break Free From Father Wounds & Emotional Damage

Unhealed wounds distort your identity and your view of God.

OPENING PRAYER

Father, in Jesus' name, I bring You every wound I've buried, ignored, or tried to outgrow without healing. I repent for letting pain shape my identity and distort how I see You. Holy Spirit, heal what is broken in me, restore truth in me, and lead me into wholeness. Amen.

THE ISSUE

Father wounds don't just hurt emotionally. They shape how you live spiritually. If your earthly father was absent, harsh, inconsistent, abusive, or passive, that damage can rewrite your expectations of God.

It can make you feel unwanted, unsafe, rejected, or like love must be earned. And if you don't confront it, you'll keep reacting like a wounded child while trying to live like a mature believer.

WHY IT'S HAPPENING

- You're still carrying pain you never processed in truth.
- You've built defenses instead of letting God heal the root.
- You've made inner vows ("I'll never trust," "I'll never need anyone," "I must perform to be loved").
- You've projected your father's failures onto God.
- You've survived, but you haven't been restored.

WHERE IT CAME FROM

These wounds often started early through neglect, abandonment, criticism, violence, addiction, divorce, betrayal, or emotional absence. Even if the father was present, the love may have been inconsistent, conditional, or cold.

The root is rejection and pain, but the door stays open when you keep replaying the injury, avoiding vulnerability, and living from self-protection. And the lie underneath it sounds like this: "I'm not worth staying for, and God won't be different." That lie is deep, but Jesus came to uproot it.

BREAK FREE DECLARATION

I break agreement with rejection, abandonment, and emotional damage in the name of Jesus Christ.
I reject the lie that I am unwanted, unprotected, or unloved.
Jesus is Lord over my past, my pain, and my identity.
I forgive what must be forgiven, and I release what must be released.
I receive healing, sonship, and restoration through the Father's love.

SCRIPTURE-BACKED DECREES

1. God is not like broken men. I declare that my Father in heaven is good, according to Psalm 100:5, "For Yahweh is good. His loving kindness endures forever."

2. I am not abandoned. I decree that even if people failed me, God will receive me, according to Psalm 27:10, "When my father and my mother forsake me, then Yahweh will take me up."

3. I am wanted by God. I declare that the Father chose me in Christ, according to Ephesians 1:4, "He chose us in him before the foundation of the world."

4. I belong in the family of God. I decree that I have been adopted by the Father, according to Ephesians 1:5, "having predestined us for adoption as children through Jesus Christ."

5. My identity is not rejection. I declare that I am accepted in Christ, according to Ephesians 1:6, "he freely gave us favor in the Beloved."

6. The Father's love is not earned. It is given. I decree that the Father has loved me first, according to 1 John 4:19, "We love him because he first loved us."

7. I am not fatherless in the Kingdom. I declare that God is a Father to the fatherless, according to Psalm 68:5, "A father of the fatherless… is God in his holy habitation."

8. God is not distant from my pain. I decree that He is near to the brokenhearted, according to Psalm 34:18, "Yahweh is near to those who have a broken heart."

9. I will not be led by trauma responses. I declare that God gives me self-control, according to 2 Timothy 1:7, "God didn't give us a spirit of fear, but of power, love, and self-control."

10. My past does not have authority over my future. I decree that I am a new creation in Christ, according to 2 Corinthians 5:17, "The old things have passed away."

11. I do not have to stay wounded to survive. I declare that God heals the brokenhearted, according to Psalm 147:3, "He heals the brokenhearted, and binds up their wounds."

12. God restores what was damaged. I decree that the Lord restores my soul, according to Psalm 23:3, "He restores my soul."

13. I will not live defined by shame. I declare that the Lord removes condemnation in Christ, according to Romans 8:1, "There is therefore now no condemnation to those who are in Christ Jesus."

14. God's love is stable, not unpredictable. I decree that His loving kindness is everlasting, according to Jeremiah 31:3, "Yes, I have loved you with an everlasting love."

15. I don't have to perform to be loved. I declare that salvation is by grace, according to Ephesians 2:8–9, "by grace you have been saved… not of works."

16. God is gentle with my weakness. I decree that Jesus does not crush the bruised, according to Isaiah 42:3, "He won't break a bruised reed."

17. I can trust God with my heart again. I declare that God is faithful and cannot lie, according to Numbers 23:19, "God is not a man, that

he should lie."

18. I can forgive without pretending it didn't hurt. I decree that I forgive because I have been forgiven, according to Colossians 3:13, "forgiving each other… even as Christ forgave you."

19. I will not carry bitterness as protection. I declare that I put away bitterness, according to Ephesians 4:31–32, "Let all bitterness… be put away from you."

20. My heart will be strengthened by God's peace. I decree that God's peace guards me, according to Philippians 4:7, "The peace of God… will guard your hearts and your thoughts."

21. I am truly known by God. I declare that the Lord knows me completely, according to Psalm 139:1, "Yahweh, you have searched me, and you know me."

22. I am not disqualified by my upbringing. I decree that God works all things for good, according to Romans 8:28, "all things work together for good."

23. God's presence stays with me. I declare that the Lord will not leave me, according to Hebrews 13:5, "I will in no way leave you."

24. I will live as a son, not as an orphan. I decree that I cry, "Abba, Father," by the Spirit, according to Romans 8:15, "you received the Spirit of adoption, by whom we cry, 'Abba! Father!'"

25. The Father's house is open to me. I declare that the Father receives the returning son, according to Luke 15:20, "his father saw him, and was moved with compassion… and kissed him."

OBEDIENCE ACTIVATION

Confession

Jesus, I repent for letting pain shape my identity, and I receive the Father's healing and love.

Action Steps

- Name the wound honestly and stop pretending it didn't affect you.
- Forgive what must be forgiven without excusing what was wrong.
- Replace the father-lie by speaking 3 decrees every day for the next 7 days.
- Bring it into the light by talking with a pastor or mature believer about what I've carried.
- Practice sonship daily by praying, "Father, show me Your love today," and listening.

Accountability Move

Today, I will reach out to one trusted believer and say, "I need prayer for healing from father wounds."

CLOSING PRAYER

Father, in Jesus' name, I bring You my pain, my history, and every place where rejection has shaped me. I repent for believing lies about myself and for projecting human failure onto Your character. I forgive what I need to forgive, and I release the weight I was never meant to carry. Holy Spirit, heal the broken places, restore my identity, and teach me to live as a loved son. I declare that You are good, You are near, and You are faithful to finish Your work in me. In the name of Jesus, amen.

CHAPTER 7

Break Free From Low Identity & Self-Rejection

You can't walk in authority while you hate who God made.

OPENING PRAYER

Father, in Jesus' name, I repent for agreeing with self-hatred, insecurity, and every lie against my identity. I renounce the belief that I am less than, forgotten, or disqualified. Holy Spirit, rebuild my identity in truth and teach me to see myself the way You see me. Amen.

THE ISSUE

Low identity isn't just "low confidence." It's a spiritual agreement with lies. It's living like you're a mistake, an afterthought, or a burden; while trying to follow Jesus with authority. Self-rejection makes you shrink, hide, delay, and sabotage what God called you to build. And if you hate who God made, you will never fully step into what God assigned.

WHY IT'S HAPPENING

- You've been measuring your worth by performance instead of sonship.
- You've internalized rejection from people and treated it as truth.
- You keep replaying failure and calling it "humility."
- You've compared yourself to others and despised your design.
- You're letting your feelings define you more than Scripture.

WHERE IT CAME FROM

Self-rejection often begins early: criticism, bullying, abandonment, betrayal, never feeling chosen, or constantly being told you weren't enough. It can also start after a major failure, addiction, or sin that made you feel stained.

The root is usually rejection and shame, but the door stays open through self-talk, isolation, and agreement with lies. And the lie underneath it sounds

like this: "God may love me, but He doesn't actually want me." That lie
keeps believers saved but powerless.

BREAK FREE DECLARATION

I break agreement with low identity, insecurity, and self-rejection in the
name of Jesus Christ.
I reject the lie that I am unwanted, unworthy, or disqualified from purpose.
Jesus is Lord over my mind, my emotions, and my identity.
I receive my identity as a son of God, made new in Christ.
I will walk in obedience, confidence, and authority because I belong to Him.

SCRIPTURE-BACKED DECREES

1. I am not a mistake. I declare that God formed me intentionally,
   according to Psalm 139:13–14, "For you formed my inmost being.
   You knit me together in my mother's womb… I am fearfully and
   wonderfully made."

2. God's design in me is not flawed. I decree that I am wonderfully
   made by God, according to Psalm 139:14, "I am fearfully and
   wonderfully made."

3. My worth is not based on performance. I declare that I am saved by
   grace, not by works, according to Ephesians 2:8–9, "For by grace
   you have been saved… not of works."

4. I belong to God completely. I decree that I was bought with a price,
   according to 1 Corinthians 6:20, "For you were bought with a
   price."

5. I am accepted in Christ. I declare that God freely gave me favor in
   Jesus, according to Ephesians 1:6, "he freely gave us favor in the
   Beloved."

6. I am chosen by God. I decree that God chose me in Christ,
   according to Ephesians 1:4, "He chose us in him before the
   foundation of the world."

7. I am not disqualified by my past. I declare that I am a new creation

in Christ, according to 2 Corinthians 5:17, "The old things have passed away."

8. My identity is in Christ, not in sin. I decree that I have been made new, according to 2 Corinthians 5:17, "Behold, all things have become new."

9. I am not abandoned. I declare that the Lord will not leave me, according to Hebrews 13:5, "I will in no way leave you, neither will I in any way forsake you."

10. I am deeply loved by God. I decree that God loved me while I was still a sinner, according to Romans 5:8, "But God commends his own love toward us… while we were yet sinners, Christ died for us."

11. God's love is not fragile. I declare that nothing can separate me from God's love, according to Romans 8:38–39, "nothing… will be able to separate us from the love of God."

12. I do not have to stay stuck in shame. I decree that there is no condemnation for me in Christ, according to Romans 8:1, "There is therefore now no condemnation."

13. My mind will be renewed in truth. I declare that I am transformed by renewing my mind, according to Romans 12:2, "be transformed by the renewing of your mind."

14. I am not powerless. I decree that God gave me power, love, and self-control, according to 2 Timothy 1:7, "God didn't give us a spirit of fear."

15. God is shaping me for purpose. I declare that I am God's workmanship, according to Ephesians 2:10, "For we are his workmanship, created in Christ Jesus for good works."

16. God prepared an assignment for me. I decree that God prepared good works for me to walk in, according to Ephesians 2:10, "which God prepared before that we should walk in them."

17. I will not despise the process. I declare that God honors small

beginnings, according to Zechariah 4:10, "For who despises the day of small things?"

18. God is not finished with me. I decree that God will complete what He started, according to Philippians 1:6, "he who began a good work in you will complete it."

19. I am part of the body of Christ. I declare that I belong and I am needed, according to 1 Corinthians 12:18, "But now God has set the members, each one of them, in the body, just as he desired."

20. I will not curse myself with my words. I decree that life and death are in the power of the tongue, according to Proverbs 18:21, "Death and life are in the power of the tongue."

21. My words will align with God's truth. I declare that I will speak truth over my life, according to Psalm 19:14, "Let the words of my mouth… be acceptable in your sight."

22. I will walk in confidence through Christ. I decree that I can do what God calls me to do through Christ, according to Philippians 4:13, "I can do all things through Christ, who strengthens me."

23. God gives me strength for obedience. I declare that the Lord strengthens me, according to Isaiah 41:10, "I will strengthen you. Yes, I will help you."

24. I will live as a son, not as an orphan. I decree that I received the Spirit of adoption, according to Romans 8:15, "you received the Spirit of adoption, by whom we cry, 'Abba! Father!'"

OBEDIENCE ACTIVATION

Confession

Jesus, I repent for rejecting myself, and I receive my identity as a son of God in Christ.

Action Steps

- Stop self-insulting language and replace it with Scripture-backed truth every day.
- Speak 3 decrees out loud daily for the next 7 days, even if it feels unnatural.
- Write down the lie you've believed ("I'm not enough") and replace it with one verse.
- Take one obedient step today toward what God called you to do. No shrinking back.
- Get around mature believers who strengthen identity instead of feeding insecurity.

Accountability Move

Today, I will tell one trusted believer, "I'm battling low identity. Help me stay anchored in truth."

CLOSING PRAYER

Father, in Jesus' name, I repent for rejecting myself and believing lies about who I am. I renounce insecurity, self-hatred, and every agreement with shame and disqualification. Holy Spirit, renew my mind, rebuild my confidence in truth, and teach me to live as a loved son. I receive Your love, Your calling, and Your strength for obedience. I declare that my identity is in Christ, and I will walk in authority without shrinking back. In the name of Jesus, amen.

CHAPTER 8

Break Free From People-Pleasing & Fear of Man

Approval becomes a prison when you're addicted to being liked.

OPENING PRAYER

Father, in Jesus' name, I repent for fearing people more than I fear You. I renounce the need for approval and the desire to be liked at the cost of obedience. Holy Spirit, strengthen my spine, purify my motives, and teach me to live for the Lord alone. Amen.

THE ISSUE

People-pleasing is not kindness. It's bondage. It's adjusting your convictions to keep relationships, staying silent to avoid conflict, and choosing comfort over obedience.

Fear of man makes you hesitate, shrink back, and ignore what God told you to do. And when approval becomes your fuel, you will always be controlled by whoever withholds it.

WHY IT'S HAPPENING

- You're craving acceptance instead of standing secure in sonship.
- You've trained yourself to avoid discomfort and confrontation.
- You're afraid of being misunderstood, rejected, or criticized.
- You're addicted to peace with people instead of peace with God.
- You're confusing "love" with "compromise."

WHERE IT CAME FROM

Fear of man often starts early: rejection, bullying, performance-based love, harsh authority, or growing up needing to keep the peace to feel safe. Over time, you learned to read the room, adjust yourself, and earn approval by staying agreeable.

The root is insecurity, but the door stays open through silence, compromise, and constant need for validation. And the lie underneath it sounds like this: "If they don't approve of me, I'll lose something I can't survive without." That lie keeps believers quiet when heaven is calling them to stand.

BREAK FREE DECLARATION

I break agreement with people-pleasing and fear of man in the name of Jesus Christ.
I reject the lie that I need approval to be secure or obedience to be safe.
Jesus is Lord over my reputation, my relationships, and my decisions.
I choose truth over comfort, conviction over applause, and obedience over acceptance.
I will fear God, stand firm, and live free.

SCRIPTURE-BACKED DECREES

1. Fear of man will not control me. I declare that fearing people is a trap, according to Proverbs 29:25, "The fear of man proves to be a snare."

2. My safety is in the Lord, not in approval. I decree that trusting in Yahweh makes me secure, according to Proverbs 29:25, "But whoever puts his trust in Yahweh will be safe."

3. I will not be ashamed of Jesus. I declare that I will confess Christ boldly, according to Romans 1:16, "For I am not ashamed of the Good News of Christ."

4. I will not live for human applause. I decree that I seek God's approval first, according to Galatians 1:10, "If I were still trying to please men, I wouldn't be a servant of Christ."

5. I am called to serve Christ, not impress people. I declare that I am a servant of Jesus, according to Galatians 1:10, "I wouldn't be a servant of Christ."

6. I will obey God even when it costs me. I decree that obedience belongs to God above man, according to Acts 5:29, "We must obey God rather than men."

7. God's opinion is greater than human opinion. I declare that the Lord looks at the heart, according to 1 Samuel 16:7, "Yahweh doesn't see as man sees… but Yahweh looks at the heart."

8. I will not shrink back in fear. I decree that God did not give me a spirit of fear, according to 2 Timothy 1:7, "For God didn't give us a spirit of fear, but of power, love, and self-control."

9. I carry power to stand firm. I declare that God has given me power, according to 2 Timothy 1:7, "but of power…"

10. Love does not require compromise. I decree that love rejoices with truth, according to 1 Corinthians 13:6, "doesn't rejoice in unrighteousness, but rejoices with the truth."

11. I will speak truth in love without fear. I declare that God calls me to speak truth, according to Ephesians 4:15, "speaking truth in love."

12. My life will be led by the Spirit, not the crowd. I decree that I am led by the Spirit of God, according to Romans 8:14, "For as many as are led by the Spirit of God, these are children of God."

13. My identity is secure in Christ. I declare that I am accepted in the Beloved, according to Ephesians 1:6, "he freely gave us favor in the Beloved."

14. Rejection from people does not cancel God's calling. I decree that God chose me, according to John 15:16, "You didn't choose me, but I chose you."

15. I will not be double-minded to keep approval. I declare that double-mindedness produces instability, according to James 1:8, "He is a double-minded man, unstable in all his ways."

16. God strengthens me when I stand. I decree that the Lord helps me, according to Isaiah 41:10, "I will strengthen you. Yes, I will help you."

17. I will not fear what people can do to me. I declare that the Lord is my helper, according to Hebrews 13:6, "The Lord is my helper. I

will not fear.”

18. My confidence is rooted in the Lord. I decree that God is with me always, according to Matthew 28:20, “behold, I am with you always.”

19. I will not trade conviction for comfort. I declare that friendship with the world is hostility toward God, according to James 4:4, “friendship with the world is enmity with God.”

20. I will not be conformed to pressure. I decree that I will be transformed by renewing my mind, according to Romans 12:2, “Don’t be conformed to this world.”

21. I will honor God openly and without shame. I declare that whoever confesses Jesus, He will confess them, according to Matthew 10:32, “Everyone therefore who confesses me before men… I will also confess him.”

22. God rewards obedience, not popularity. I decree that the Lord sees what is done in secret, according to Matthew 6:4, “your Father who sees in secret will reward you.”

23. I will be courageous when truth is unpopular. I declare that the Lord commands me to be strong, according to Joshua 1:9, “Be strong and courageous… for Yahweh your God is with you.”

24. I will live to please God alone. I decree that my life belongs to the Lord, according to Romans 14:8, “if we live, we live to the Lord.”

OBEDIENCE ACTIVATION

Confession

Jesus, I repent for fearing people more than You, and I surrender my reputation to Your lordship.

Action Steps

- Identify one area of compromise where you’ve been staying silent to keep approval.

- Obey immediately in the next moment God convicts you. No delay. No negotiation.
- Practice truth-telling by saying one hard but loving truth this week.
- Stop chasing validation by limiting social approval habits and people-pleasing patterns.
- Speak 3 decrees daily for the next 7 days to rebuild backbone and courage.

Accountability Move

Today, I will tell one trusted believer, "I'm breaking fear of man. Hold me to obedience."

CLOSING PRAYER

Father, in Jesus' name, I repent for fearing rejection and craving approval more than obedience. I renounce people-pleasing, compromise, and the need to be liked. Holy Spirit, strengthen me to stand firm, speak truth in love, and follow Jesus without hesitation. I surrender my reputation, relationships, and decisions to the lordship of Christ. I declare that I will fear God, walk in courage, and live free. In the name of Jesus, amen.

CHAPTER 9

Break Free From Unforgiveness & Bitterness

Bitterness is poison you drink hoping they die.

OPENING PRAYER

Father, in Jesus' name, I come to You with every wound I've held onto and every offense I've replayed. I repent for letting bitterness live in my heart and call it protection. Holy Spirit, soften me, cleanse me, and lead me into forgiveness and freedom. Amen.

THE ISSUE

Unforgiveness isn't strength. It's bondage. Bitterness is what happens when pain goes untreated and offense becomes a lifestyle. It keeps wounds open, relationships strained, prayer powerless, and joy inaccessible. And the longer you hold onto it, the more it feels normal until bitterness becomes your personality.

WHY IT'S HAPPENING

- You keep replaying what they did instead of releasing it to God.
- You've confused forgiveness with excusing the offense.
- You're waiting for them to feel what you felt before you let it go.
- You've made pain your identity and anger your protection.
- You've been holding a debt only God can judge rightly.

WHERE IT CAME FROM

Bitterness usually starts with real injury: betrayal, abandonment, abuse, humiliation, injustice, or repeated disrespect. The root is pain, but the door stays open when I keep rehearsing the offense, feeding resentment, and refusing release.

Over time, unforgiveness becomes a prison you live in while the other person keeps living. And the lie underneath it sounds like this: "If I forgive, they win and I lose." But forgiveness is not their reward. It's your freedom.

BREAK FREE DECLARATION

I break agreement with unforgiveness, bitterness, and resentment in the name of Jesus Christ.
I reject the lie that holding onto offense keeps me safe or makes me strong.
Jesus is Lord over my heart, my pain, and my healing process.
I release every debt, every offense, and every injustice into the hands of God.
I choose forgiveness, cleansing, and freedom, and I will not carry poison anymore.

SCRIPTURE-BACKED DECREES

1. Bitterness will not live in me. I declare that I put away bitterness, according to Ephesians 4:31, "Let all bitterness, wrath, anger, outcry, and slander, be put away from you, with all malice."

2. My heart will be clean, not contaminated. I decree that I choose kindness and forgiveness, according to Ephesians 4:32, "Be kind to one another… forgiving each other, just as God also in Christ forgave you."

3. I forgive because I have been forgiven. I declare that Christ forgave me, according to Colossians 3:13, "forgiving each other… even as Christ forgave you."

4. I will not hold debts in my spirit. I decree that I release offenses as the Lord commands, according to Colossians 3:13, "if anyone has a complaint… forgive each other."

5. Unforgiveness will not block my prayers. I declare that I forgive when I stand praying, according to Mark 11:25, "when you stand praying, forgive, if you have anything against anyone."

6. I will not imprison myself to punish another person. I decree that forgiveness is my obedience, according to Mark 11:25, "so that your Father… may also forgive you."

7. Vengeance belongs to God, not me. I declare that I release justice into the Lord's hands, according to Romans 12:19, "Vengeance belongs to me; I will repay, says the Lord."

8. I will not repay evil with evil. I decree that I overcome evil with good, according to Romans 12:21, "Don't be overcome by evil, but overcome evil with good."

9. My healing matters to God. I declare that the Lord heals the brokenhearted, according to Psalm 147:3, "He heals the brokenhearted, and binds up their wounds."

10. God sees what happened to me. I decree that the Lord is near to the crushed, according to Psalm 34:18, "Yahweh is near to those who have a broken heart."

11. My soul will not stay trapped in resentment. I declare that the Lord restores my soul, according to Psalm 23:3, "He restores my soul."

12. I will not let offense grow into a root. I decree that bitterness will not take root in me, according to Hebrews 12:15, "lest any root of bitterness springing up trouble you."

13. Bitterness will not trouble my life anymore. I declare that I will live free from a bitter root, according to Hebrews 12:15, "and thereby many be defiled."

14. I will guard my heart with wisdom. I decree that my heart is protected, according to Proverbs 4:23, "Keep your heart with all diligence, for out of it is the wellspring of life."

15. I will not be controlled by anger. I declare that I am slow to anger by God's wisdom, according to Proverbs 14:29, "He who is slow to anger has great understanding."

16. I choose mercy over revenge. I decree that mercy triumphs over judgment, according to James 2:13, "Mercy triumphs over judgment."

17. I will bless instead of curse. I declare that I bless those who wrong me, according to Luke 6:28, "bless those who curse you, and pray

for those who mistreat you."

18. I will pray for my enemies in obedience. I decree that I love my enemies as Jesus commands, according to Matthew 5:44, "Love your enemies… and pray for those who persecute you."

19. I will forgive from the heart, not just with words. I declare that I forgive sincerely, according to Matthew 18:35, "So my heavenly Father will also do to you, if you don't each forgive your brother from your hearts."

20. I release control and trust God's justice. I decree that the Lord judges righteously, according to 1 Peter 2:23, "but committed himself to him who judges righteously."

21. I will not carry what Jesus already carried. I declare that Christ bore my burdens and sins, according to 1 Peter 2:24, "who his own self bore our sins in his body on the tree."

22. The Holy Spirit empowers my obedience. I decree that God gives me power and self-control, according to 2 Timothy 1:7, "but of power, love, and self-control."

23. My peace is worth protecting. I declare that God's peace guards my heart, according to Philippians 4:7, "The peace of God… will guard your hearts and your thoughts."

24. Love will lead me, not offense. I decree that love is not resentful, according to 1 Corinthians 13:5, "doesn't take account of evil."

OBEDIENCE ACTIVATION

Confession

Jesus, I repent for holding onto bitterness, and I choose to forgive as I have been forgiven.

Action Steps

- Name the person and the offense honestly before God instead of pretending it didn't matter.

- Release the debt out loud: "I forgive ___ for ___, and I release them to God."
- Refuse the replay by cutting off mental rehearsals the moment they start.
- Bless them in prayer for 7 days, not because they deserve it, but because you need freedom.
- Seek counsel if needed when the wound is deep or traumatic. Healing is still obedience.

Accountability Move

Today, I will tell one trusted believer, "I'm choosing forgiveness. Pray with me so I don't go back."

CLOSING PRAYER

Father, in Jesus' name, I bring You my pain, my anger, and every offense I've carried. I repent for holding bitterness in my heart and calling it protection. I choose to forgive, and I release every debt into Your hands as the righteous Judge. Holy Spirit, cleanse my heart, heal what was wounded, and teach me to walk in peace. I declare that bitterness will not rule me, and unforgiveness will not poison me anymore. In the name of Jesus, amen.

CHAPTER 10

Break Free From Offense Culture & Being Easily Triggered

Being constantly offended is a distraction dressed as discernment.

OPENING PRAYER

Father, in Jesus' name, I repent for being easily offended, reactive, and quick to judge. I renounce pride, anger, and the need to be "right" at the cost of peace and love. Holy Spirit, train my heart, guard my mouth, and teach me to walk in maturity. Amen.

THE ISSUE

Living offended feels like strength, but it's actually bondage. It keeps you irritated, suspicious, defensive, and constantly on edge. It turns every disagreement into an attack and every correction into betrayal. And when offense becomes your default setting, you stop building the Kingdom and start fighting people.

WHY IT'S HAPPENING

- You're reacting from pride instead of responding with humility.
- You've confused being easily offended with being spiritually "aware."
- You're addicted to conflict and calling it "conviction."
- You're carrying unresolved wounds that make everything feel personal.
- You're speaking too quickly and listening too little.

WHERE IT CAME FROM

Offense often comes from insecurity, unhealed rejection, or a deep need to control the narrative.
Sometimes it started after betrayal, church hurt, or repeated disrespect, where you learned to stay guarded.

The root is often pride mixed with pain, but the door stays open through constant reaction, suspicion, and judgment.

And the lie underneath it sounds like this: "If I stay offended, I stay protected." But offense doesn't protect you. It poisons you.

BREAK FREE DECLARATION

I break agreement with offense, irritation, and reactivity in the name of Jesus Christ.
I reject the lie that being easily offended makes me strong, discerning, or safe.
Jesus is Lord over my emotions, my reactions, and my relationships.
I choose maturity, humility, and peace, and I will not be controlled by my triggers.
I will build, not bite. I will bless, not burn.

SCRIPTURE-BACKED DECREES

1. Offense will not rule my spirit. I declare that I will be slow to anger, according to James 1:19, "Let every man be swift to hear, slow to speak, and slow to anger."

2. I will not confuse anger with righteousness. I decree that the anger of man does not produce God's righteousness, according to James 1:20, "For the anger of man doesn't produce the righteousness of God."

3. My mouth will not run ahead of wisdom. I declare that I will be slow to speak, according to James 1:19, "slow to speak."

4. I will respond with gentleness instead of reaction. I decree that a gentle answer turns away wrath, according to Proverbs 15:1, "A gentle answer turns away wrath."

5. I will not live quarrelsome and loud. I declare that wisdom is peaceable and gentle, according to James 3:17, "the wisdom that is from above is first pure, then peaceable, gentle."

6. My discernment will be clean, not cynical. I decree that heavenly

wisdom is full of mercy, according to James 3:17, "full of mercy and good fruits."

7. I will not be controlled by irritation. I declare that love is patient and kind, according to 1 Corinthians 13:4, "Love is patient and is kind."

8. I will not keep score in my heart. I decree that love does not keep a record of wrongs, according to 1 Corinthians 13:5, "doesn't take account of evil."

9. My heart will stay guarded, not hardened. I declare that I keep my heart with diligence, according to Proverbs 4:23, "Keep your heart with all diligence, for out of it is the wellspring of life."

10. I will refuse the trap of constant conflict. I decree that a fool vents anger but a wise man holds it back, according to Proverbs 29:11, "A fool vents all of his anger, but a wise man brings himself under control."

11. I will not return insult for insult. I declare that I bless instead of retaliate, according to 1 Peter 3:9, "not paying back evil for evil... but, on the contrary, blessing."

12. My words will build, not destroy. I decree that I speak what gives grace, according to Ephesians 4:29, "let no corrupt speech proceed out of your mouth... that it may give grace."

13. Bitterness will not hide behind my "opinions." I declare that I put away bitterness and wrath, according to Ephesians 4:31, "Let all bitterness, wrath, anger... be put away from you."

14. I will live tenderhearted, not triggered. I decree that I choose kindness and forgiveness, according to Ephesians 4:32, "Be kind to one another, tenderhearted, forgiving each other."

15. I will pursue peace on purpose. I declare that I seek peace and follow it, according to Psalm 34:14, "Seek peace, and pursue it."

16. Pride will not lead my reactions. I decree that God resists the proud but gives grace to the humble, according to James 4:6, "God resists the proud, but gives grace to the humble."

17. Humility will be my posture. I declare that I humble myself under God's hand, according to 1 Peter 5:6, "Humble yourselves therefore

under the mighty hand of God."

18. I will not be quick to accuse motives. I decree that love believes the best and endures, according to 1 Corinthians 13:7, "bears all things, believes all things, hopes all things."

19. I will be peacemaking, not drama-making. I declare that peacemakers are blessed, according to Matthew 5:9, "Blessed are the peacemakers."

20. I will control my spirit instead of being controlled. I decree that ruling my spirit is strength, according to Proverbs 16:32, "He who rules his spirit is better than he who takes a city."

21. I will not let offense become a doorway to sin. I declare that anger must not give the devil a place, according to Ephesians 4:26–27, "Don't let the sun go down on your wrath, and don't give place to the devil."

22. I will forgive quickly instead of holding grudges. I decree that I forgive as Christ forgave me, according to Colossians 3:13, "forgiving each other... even as Christ forgave you."

23. I will live led by the Spirit, not by my feelings. I declare that those led by the Spirit are God's children, according to Romans 8:14, "For as many as are led by the Spirit of God, these are children of God."

24. My life will reflect Jesus, not my triggers. I decree that the fruit of the Spirit will grow in me, according to Galatians 5:22–23, "the fruit of the Spirit is love, joy, peace... self-control."

OBEDIENCE ACTIVATION

Confession

Jesus, I repent for being easily offended, reactive, and prideful, and I surrender my emotions to You.

Action Steps

- Pause before responding and pray silently before speaking when you feel triggered.

- Ask, "Is this worth losing peace over?" before you argue or clap back.
- Stop feeding outrage content that keeps you irritated and reactive.
- Seek reconciliation quickly when offense rises instead of letting it ferment.
- Speak 3 decrees daily for 7 days to retrain your reactions.

Accountability Move

Today, I will tell one trusted believer, "I'm breaking offense. Help me stay mature and peaceful."

CLOSING PRAYER

Father, in Jesus' name, I repent for pride, reactivity, and living easily offended. I renounce bitterness, irritation, and every trigger that keeps me distracted and divided. Holy Spirit, teach me to be slow to speak, quick to listen, and quick to forgive. Guard my mouth, train my emotions, and make me a peacemaker with maturity. I declare that offense will not rule me, and I will walk in humility, peace, and love. In the name of Jesus, amen.

CHAPTER 11

Break Free From Religious Performance

Busy for God, but not surrendered to God.

OPENING PRAYER

Father, in Jesus' name, I repent for doing Christian things without living surrendered to You. I renounce performance, appearance, and empty routine. Holy Spirit, purify my motives, revive my heart, and lead me into real obedience. Amen.

THE ISSUE

Religious performance looks like devotion, but it can be dead inside. It's serving, posting, attending, volunteering, and staying "busy for God" while your heart stays unchanged. It's an external activity without internal surrender. And if you don't break it, you can look spiritual in public while staying powerless in private.

WHY IT'S HAPPENING

- You've replaced intimacy with activity.
- You've learned how to look right without living right.
- You're chasing approval and calling it "ministry."
- You're avoiding repentance by staying busy.
- You've trained your life to perform instead of obey.

WHERE IT CAME FROM

Religious performance often begins when you believe God is pleased with you because you're active. Not because you're obedient. The root is usually fear of being "not enough," mixed with pride and the need to appear strong.

The door stays open when you keep doing religious routines while resisting conviction and avoiding surrender. And the lie underneath it sounds like this: "If I look faithful, I am faithful." But appearance is not obedience.

BREAK FREE DECLARATION

I break agreement with religious performance and false spirituality in the name of Jesus Christ.
I reject the lie that activity equals surrender and routine equals relationship.
Jesus is Lord over my heart, my motives, and my obedience.
I choose repentance over image and intimacy over performance.
I will obey God in secret, not just appear spiritual in public.

SCRIPTURE-BACKED DECREES

1. God wants my heart, not my act. I declare that God looks at the heart, according to 1 Samuel 16:7, "Man looks at the outward appearance, but Yahweh looks at the heart."

2. External appearance is not the measure of obedience. I decree that true worship begins inwardly, according to John 4:24, "God is spirit, and those who worship him must worship in spirit and truth."

3. Empty words do not impress God. I declare that people can honor God with lips while their heart is far, according to Matthew 15:8, "These people honor me with their lips, but their heart is far from me."

4. Routine without surrender is useless. I decree that worship without obedience is vain, according to Matthew 15:9, "But in vain do they worship me."

5. God desires obedience over sacrifice. I declare that obedience matters more than religious activity, according to 1 Samuel 15:22, "To obey is better than sacrifice."

6. I will not substitute serving for surrender. I decree that I will present my body as a living sacrifice, according to Romans 12:1, "present your bodies a living sacrifice… which is your spiritual service."

7. I am called to be transformed, not just informed. I declare that I will be renewed in my mind, according to Romans 12:2, "be transformed by the renewing of your mind."

8. God is not pleased by hypocrisy. I decree that He hates a divided

life, according to Isaiah 29:13, "their fear of me is a commandment of men which has been taught."

9. Private holiness matters to God. I declare that God sees in secret, according to Matthew 6:6, "your Father who sees in secret will reward you."

10. God is not after my image. He's after my obedience. I decree that hearing without doing is deception, according to James 1:22, "be doers of the word, and not only hearers."

11. Religious activity without love is empty. I declare that without love, I gain nothing, according to 1 Corinthians 13:3, "but don't have love, it profits me nothing."

12. I will not hide behind religion while resisting repentance. I decree that godly sorrow produces repentance, according to 2 Corinthians 7:10, "godly sorrow produces repentance leading to salvation."

13. Jesus must be Lord, not a topic. I declare that saying "Lord" without obedience is unacceptable, according to Luke 6:46, "Why do you call me, 'Lord, Lord,' and don't do the things which I say?"

14. My faith must produce fruit. I decree that real belief produces obedience, according to James 2:17, "faith, if it has no works, is dead in itself."

15. I will not be busy while spiritually barren. I declare that remaining in Jesus produces fruit, according to John 15:5, "He who remains in me… bears much fruit."

16. God is not interested in my excuses. I decree that He desires truth in the inward parts, according to Psalm 51:6, "Behold, you desire truth in the inward parts."

17. I will live clean on the inside. I declare that God cleanses me when I confess, according to 1 John 1:9, "to cleanse us from all unrighteousness."

18. I will not perform righteousness for attention. I decree that God warns against public show, according to Matthew 6:1, "be careful

that you don't do your charitable giving before men."

19. Humility is the posture of true discipleship. I declare that God gives grace to the humble, according to James 4:6, "God resists the proud, but gives grace to the humble."

20. I am not called to impress people. I decree that seeking man's approval is not servanthood, according to Galatians 1:10, "If I were still trying to please men, I wouldn't be a servant of Christ."

21. God delights in truth, not performance. I declare that the Lord examines me, according to Psalm 139:23, "Search me, God, and know my heart."

22. My worship must include obedience. I decree that I offer my life to God, according to Colossians 3:23, "Whatever you do, work heartily, as for the Lord."

23. I will live for eternity, not applause. I declare that God will judge what is done, according to 2 Corinthians 5:10, "For we must all be revealed before the judgment seat of Christ."

24. God is worthy of my whole life. I decree that I deny myself and follow Jesus daily, according to Luke 9:23, "let him deny himself, take up his cross daily, and follow me."

OBEDIENCE ACTIVATION

Confession

Jesus, I repent for religious performance, and I surrender my heart fully to You as Lord.

Action Steps

- Identify one area where you look spiritual but resist obedience and repent specifically.
- Spend time with God without producing anything. No posting, no performing, just prayer and Scripture.
- Obey one clear conviction immediately today instead of delaying.

- Remove a "busy" distraction that keeps you from real intimacy with God.
- Speak 3 decrees daily for 7 days to retrain your motives and rebuild surrender.

Accountability Move

Today, I will tell one trusted believer, "Pray for me. I want surrender, not performance."

CLOSING PRAYER

Father, in Jesus' name, I repent for activity without intimacy and appearance without obedience. I renounce religious performance, hypocrisy, and every attempt to impress people instead of honoring You. Holy Spirit, purify my motives, bring me into true repentance, and teach me to obey in secret. I surrender my heart, my schedule, and my life to Jesus Christ as Lord. I declare that my faith will be real, my obedience will be consistent, and my devotion will be wholehearted. In the name of Jesus, amen.

CHAPTER 12

Break Free From Prayerlessness & Spiritual Neglect

If you don't pray, you don't fight.

OPENING PRAYER

Father, in Jesus' name, I repent for neglecting prayer and living like I can handle life without You. I renounce distraction, spiritual laziness, and every excuse that keeps me silent before You. Holy Spirit, awaken my spirit, strengthen my discipline, and teach me to pray with faith and consistency. Amen.

THE ISSUE

Prayerlessness is not a personality trait. It's a spiritual vulnerability. When you stop praying, you don't become neutral. You become exposed. Spiritual neglect doesn't announce itself loudly. It shows up slowly: dull conviction, weak discipline, drifting thoughts, and easy compromise. Because if you don't pray, you're not fighting. You're just surviving.

WHY IT'S HAPPENING

- You've allowed busyness to replace dependency on God.
- You've treated prayer like an option instead of a weapon.
- You've believed the lie that prayer "doesn't matter" or "doesn't work."
- You've been distracted, entertained, and mentally overloaded.
- You've been trying to win battles with willpower instead of the Spirit.

WHERE IT CAME FROM

Prayerlessness often starts with neglect, not rebellion. It begins when life gets full, disciplines get weak, and time with God gets pushed to the side. The root is usually self-reliance, but the door stays open through distraction, inconsistency, and spiritual fatigue.

And the lie underneath it sounds like this: "I'll pray later… but I'm fine right now." That lie is what keeps believers prayerless until the pressure hits.

BREAK FREE DECLARATION

I break agreement with prayerlessness and spiritual neglect in the name of Jesus Christ.
I reject the lie that I can stay strong without prayer or walk in authority without dependence.
Jesus is Lord over my time, my focus, and my spiritual life.
I choose prayer, obedience, and watchfulness over distraction and drift.
I will fight in the Spirit, not just survive in the flesh.

SCRIPTURE-BACKED DECREES

1. Prayer is not optional for a believer. I declare that I am commanded to pray without ceasing, according to 1 Thessalonians 5:17, "Pray without ceasing."

2. My spiritual strength is tied to consistent prayer. I decree that I will always pray and not give up, according to Luke 18:1, "that they must always pray, and not give up."

3. I will not drift into neglect. I declare that I stay alert and pray, according to Matthew 26:41, "Watch and pray, that you don't enter into temptation."

4. Prayer keeps me from temptation. I decree that watchfulness protects me, according to Matthew 26:41, "The spirit indeed is willing, but the flesh is weak."

5. God hears me when I call. I declare that the Lord answers when I cry out, according to Jeremiah 33:3, "Call to me, and I will answer you."

6. Prayer brings peace into my mind. I decree that anxiety breaks when I pray, according to Philippians 4:6, "In nothing be anxious… by prayer… let your requests be made known to God."

7. God's peace guards me through prayer. I declare that peace protects my heart, according to Philippians 4:7, "The peace of God… will guard your hearts and your thoughts."

8. I am called to seek God early and often. I decree that I seek God wholeheartedly, according to Jeremiah 29:13, "You shall seek me, and find me, when you shall search for me with all your heart."

9. God rewards those who seek Him. I declare that God responds to diligent seeking, according to Hebrews 11:6, "he is a rewarder of those who seek him."

10. Prayer is how I receive strength in weakness. I decree that God strengthens me, according to Isaiah 41:10, "I will strengthen you. Yes, I will help you."

11. Spiritual battles require spiritual weapons. I declare that my weapons are powerful through God, according to 2 Corinthians 10:4, "the weapons of our warfare are not of the flesh, but mighty before God."

12. I will not fight spiritual battles with flesh methods. I decree that strongholds are pulled down through God's power, according to 2 Corinthians 10:4–5, "to the throwing down of strongholds."

13. God gives wisdom when I ask. I declare that God gives wisdom generously, according to James 1:5, "let him ask of God… and it will be given to him."

14. I will not be spiritually asleep. I decree that I stay sober and watchful, according to 1 Peter 5:8, "Be sober and self-controlled. Be watchful."

15. Prayer helps me resist the devil. I declare that resistance begins with submission to God, according to James 4:7, "Be subject therefore to God. Resist the devil, and he will flee from you."

16. My time with God produces real fruit. I decree that remaining in Christ produces fruit, according to John 15:5, "He who remains in me… bears much fruit."

17. I will not neglect God's Word and prayer. I declare that the early church devoted themselves to prayer, according to Acts 2:42, "They continued steadfastly… in prayers."

18. My spirit will be strengthened by the Holy Spirit. I decree that I am strengthened with power through His Spirit, according to Ephesians 3:16, "that he would grant you… to be strengthened with power through his Spirit."

19. Prayer keeps me aligned with God's will. I declare that I pray according to His will, according to 1 John 5:14, "if we ask anything according to his will, he hears us."

20. I will not give up in prayer. I decree that I am persistent in prayer, according to Colossians 4:2, "Continue steadfastly in prayer."

21. Prayer makes me spiritually alert. I declare that I stay awake and pray, according to Luke 21:36, "Therefore be watchful all the time, praying."

22. I will be led by the Spirit, not by distraction. I decree that God leads me by His Spirit, according to Romans 8:14, "as many as are led by the Spirit of God."

23. God renews me when I depend on Him. I declare that God renews my strength, according to Isaiah 40:31, "those who wait for Yahweh will renew their strength."

24. I will build my life on dependence, not self-reliance. I decree that apart from Christ I can do nothing, according to John 15:5, "Apart from me you can do nothing."

OBEDIENCE ACTIVATION

Confession

Jesus, I repent for prayerlessness, and I surrender my time and attention back to You.

Action Steps

- Start with 5 minutes a day. No excuses, no negotiation, just prayer.
- Pray out loud to break passivity and mental drift.
- Remove one distraction that steals time with God (scrolling, late-night habits, noise).
- Use the decrees daily as your prayer language until your spirit wakes up again.
- Set a "non-negotiable" prayer window and protect it like warfare.

Accountability Move

Today, I will text one trusted believer, "Hold me to prayer. I'm rebuilding consistency."

CLOSING PRAYER

Father, in Jesus' name, I repent for spiritual neglect and trying to live strong without prayer. I renounce distraction, passivity, and the lie that prayer doesn't matter. Holy Spirit, awaken my spirit, strengthen my discipline, and teach me to pray with faith and endurance. I surrender my time, my mind, and my life to Jesus Christ as Lord. I declare that I will pray, I will fight, and I will walk in authority again. In the name of Jesus, amen.

CHAPTER 13

Break Free From Passivity & Spiritual Apathy

You believe but you're not engaged.

OPENING PRAYER

Father, in Jesus' name, I repent for passivity, apathy, and living spiritually asleep. I renounce lukewarm faith, delayed obedience, and the comfort that has numbed my spirit. Holy Spirit, wake me up, ignite hunger again, and lead me into active obedience. Amen.

THE ISSUE

Passivity is believing the right things while living like nothing is at stake. It's spiritual neutrality. No urgency, no discipline, no fight, no pursuit. Apathy makes you passive toward prayer, passive toward sin, passive toward purpose, and passive toward growth.

And a passive believer will never walk in authority because authority requires engagement.

WHY IT'S HAPPENING

- You've gotten comfortable instead of committed.
- You've been distracted and entertained into numbness.
- You've delayed obedience long enough that conviction feels quiet.
- You're consuming spiritual content without practicing spiritual obedience.
- You're waiting for motivation instead of choosing discipline.

WHERE IT CAME FROM

Passivity often begins after disappointment, burnout, unanswered prayer, or repeated failure. Sometimes you stopped fighting because you got tired of getting hurt, tired of trying, or tired of feeling like nothing changed.

The root is often discouragement, but the door stays open through comfort, distraction, and spiritual negligence. And the lie underneath it sounds like this: "Nothing really changes, so why fully engage?" But apathy isn't protection. It's surrender.

BREAK FREE DECLARATION

I break agreement with passivity, lukewarm faith, and spiritual apathy in the name of Jesus Christ.
I reject the lie that comfort is harmless and disengagement is safe.
Jesus is Lord over my focus, my discipline, and my obedience.
I choose hunger, urgency, and action instead of delay and excuses.
I will not spectate my faith. I will live it.

SCRIPTURE-BACKED DECREES

1. God did not save me to stay asleep. I declare that it is time to wake up, according to Romans 13:11, "Now it is high time for you to awake out of sleep."

2. I will not live lukewarm. I decree that Jesus rebukes lukewarm Christianity, according to Revelation 3:16, "So because you are lukewarm… I will vomit you out of my mouth."

3. Comfort will not replace conviction. I declare that Jesus calls me to repentance, according to Revelation 3:19, "As many as I love, I reprove and chasten. Be zealous therefore, and repent."

4. I will choose zeal, not apathy. I decree that I will be zealous and repent, according to Revelation 3:19, "Be zealous therefore, and repent."

5. God is not pleased with lazy faith. I declare that God desires diligence, according to Hebrews 6:12, "that you may not be sluggish, but imitators of those who through faith and patience inherited the promises."

6. I will not be spiritually sluggish. I decree that I reject spiritual laziness, according to Hebrews 6:12, "that you may not be sluggish."

7. My faith will produce action. I declare that faith without works is dead, according to James 2:17, "faith, if it has no works, is dead in itself."

8. I will not stay a hearer only. I decree that I will be a doer of the Word, according to James 1:22, "be doers of the word, and not only hearers."

9. Delayed obedience is disobedience. I declare that I obey God when He speaks, according to James 4:17, "To him therefore who knows to do good and doesn't do it, to him it is sin."

10. God strengthens me to fight again. I decree that God renews my strength, according to Isaiah 40:31, "those who wait for Yahweh will renew their strength."

11. My spirit will not stay dull. I declare that I stir up what God put in me, according to 2 Timothy 1:6, "stir up the gift of God."

12. I will not live in fear-based passivity. I decree that God gave me power, according to 2 Timothy 1:7, "God didn't give us a spirit of fear, but of power."

13. God's grace trains me to live disciplined. I declare that grace teaches me to deny ungodliness, according to Titus 2:11–12, "teaching us that… we should live soberly, righteously, and godly."

14. I will pursue God, not coast. I decree that I press on toward the goal, according to Philippians 3:14, "I press on toward the goal."

15. I will not waste my life on comfort. I declare that I redeem the time, according to Ephesians 5:16, "redeeming the time because the days are evil."

16. God calls me to spiritual strength. I decree that I am strong in the Lord, according to Ephesians 6:10, "be strong in the Lord and in the strength of his might."

17. I am built for spiritual warfare, not spiritual sleep. I declare that I put on the armor of God, according to Ephesians 6:11, "Put on the

whole armor of God."

18. I will not give the enemy easy access. I decree that I stay watchful, according to 1 Peter 5:8, "Be sober and self-controlled. Be watchful."

19. I will resist instead of retreat. I declare that resisting the devil is commanded, according to James 4:7, "Resist the devil, and he will flee from you."

20. God responds to those who draw near. I decree that I draw near to God, according to James 4:8, "Draw near to God, and he will draw near to you."

21. My life will reflect spiritual hunger. I declare that I hunger and thirst for righteousness, according to Matthew 5:6, "Blessed are those who hunger and thirst after righteousness."

22. The Holy Spirit empowers my engagement. I decree that I walk by the Spirit, according to Galatians 5:16, "Walk by the Spirit."

23. I will remain connected to Jesus daily. I declare that remaining in Christ produces fruit, according to John 15:5, "He who remains in me… bears much fruit."

24. I will not be passive about my calling. I decree that God prepared good works for me to walk in, according to Ephesians 2:10, "that we should walk in them."

25. I will finish my race with endurance. I declare that I run with perseverance, according to Hebrews 12:1, "let us run with perseverance the race that is set before us."

OBEDIENCE ACTIVATION

Confession

Jesus, I repent for passivity and apathy, and I surrender my life back to wholehearted obedience.

Action Steps

- Do one obedient thing today that you've been delaying. No excuses.
- Speak 3 decrees daily for 7 days to reignite spiritual engagement.
- Cut one comfort habit that feeds apathy (endless scrolling, late nights, passive entertainment).
- Rebuild discipline with prayer and Scripture even when motivation is absent.
- Serve and engage in your local church instead of staying disconnected.

Accountability Move

Today, I will tell one trusted believer, "I'm done coasting. Help me stay engaged and obedient."

CLOSING PRAYER

Father, in Jesus' name, I repent for lukewarm faith, spiritual passivity, and living disengaged. I renounce apathy, distraction, and every comfort that has numbed my hunger for You. Holy Spirit, wake me up, strengthen my discipline, and ignite zeal for obedience again. I surrender my time, my energy, and my focus to Jesus Christ as Lord. I declare that I will engage, I will fight, and I will build what You called me to build. In the name of Jesus, amen.

CHAPTER 14

Break Free From Comfort Addiction

Comfort is a drug, and it kills men slowly.

OPENING PRAYER

Father, in Jesus' name, I repent for choosing comfort over obedience and ease over purpose. I renounce laziness, indulgence, and every craving that keeps me spiritually dull. Holy Spirit, strengthen my discipline, sharpen my hunger, and train me to live surrendered. Amen.

THE ISSUE

Comfort addiction is when you build your life around avoiding discomfort. It's not just physical laziness. It's spiritual soft living: no urgency, no edge, no sacrifice, no discipline.

Comfort makes you passive, distracted, and numb to conviction. And over time, comfort doesn't just slow you down. It quietly replaces your calling.

WHY IT'S HAPPENING

- You've been rewarding the flesh and starving the spirit.
- You've trained your life to seek ease instead of endurance.
- You're addicted to escape (scrolling, entertainment, overeating, endless downtime).
- You avoid hard conversations and hard obedience.
- You're chasing relief instead of transformation.

WHERE IT CAME FROM

Comfort addiction often starts when pain, stress, pressure, or disappointment makes escape feel necessary. Instead of running to God, you run to whatever gives quick relief. The root is usually self-protection, but the door stays open through repeated indulgence and avoidance of hardship.

And the lie underneath it sounds like this: "I deserve comfort more than I need obedience." That lie turns believers soft while life stays hard.

BREAK FREE DECLARATION

I break agreement with comfort addiction, indulgence, and spiritual softness in the name of Jesus Christ.
I reject the lie that ease is my goal and discomfort is my enemy.
Jesus is Lord over my appetites, my schedule, and my priorities.
I choose discipline, sacrifice, and obedience over escape and indulgence.
I will live alert, strong, and useful in the Kingdom of God.

SCRIPTURE-BACKED DECREES

1. Comfort will not be my master. I declare that Jesus is Lord, according to Luke 9:23, "If anyone desires to come after me, let him deny himself, take up his cross daily, and follow me."

2. Self-denial is part of discipleship. I decree that I deny myself daily, according to Luke 9:23, "let him deny himself."

3. I was not called to an easy life. I declare that following Jesus requires surrender, according to Luke 9:23, "take up his cross daily, and follow me."

4. I will not live to please the flesh. I decree that the flesh leads to death, according to Romans 8:13, "For if you live after the flesh, you must die."

5. The Spirit leads me into life. I declare that putting to death flesh patterns brings life, according to Romans 8:13, "but if by the Spirit you put to death the deeds of the body, you will live."

6. Discipline is a weapon, not a punishment. I decree that I train myself for godliness, according to 1 Timothy 4:7, "train yourself in godliness."

7. My body will not run my life. I declare that I discipline my body, according to 1 Corinthians 9:27, "I beat my body and bring it into submission."

8. I will not be spiritually asleep. I decree that it is time to wake up, according to Romans 13:11, "Now it is high time for you to awake out of sleep."

9. Laziness will not dominate me. I declare that the sluggard comes to poverty, according to Proverbs 6:11, "So your poverty will come… and your want as an armed man."

10. Comfort will not steal my future. I decree that I sow to the Spirit, according to Galatians 6:8, "he who sows to the Spirit will reap eternal life."

11. I will not live indulgent and dull. I declare that I keep alert and sober, according to 1 Peter 5:8, "Be sober and self-controlled. Be watchful."

12. My calling requires endurance. I decree that I endure hardship, according to 2 Timothy 2:3, "You therefore must endure hardship, as a good soldier of Christ Jesus."

13. I am a soldier, not a spectator. I declare that I do not entangle myself with comfort, according to 2 Timothy 2:4, "No soldier on duty entangles himself in the affairs of life."

14. I will not trade purpose for pleasure. I decree that I set my mind on things above, according to Colossians 3:2, "Set your mind on the things that are above."

15. My appetite will not lead my obedience. I declare that God is my portion, according to Psalm 73:26, "God is the strength of my heart, and my portion forever."

16. I will choose eternal reward over temporary relief. I decree that I look at eternal things, according to 2 Corinthians 4:18, "while we don't look at the things which are seen, but at the things which are not seen."

17. I will not waste time on distractions. I declare that I redeem the time, according to Ephesians 5:16, "redeeming the time because the days are evil."

18. My comfort cannot replace obedience. I decree that I do the will of God, according to Matthew 7:21, "he who does the will of my Father who is in heaven."

19. My spirit will not be dulled by indulgence. I declare that I present my body to God, according to Romans 12:1, "present your bodies a living sacrifice."

20. Hardship can produce maturity. I decree that perseverance produces completeness, according to James 1:4, "Let perseverance have its perfect work."

21. God strengthens me to do hard things. I declare that God helps me, according to Isaiah 41:10, "I will strengthen you. Yes, I will help you."

22. I will build discipline through obedience. I decree that I do the Word, according to James 1:22, "be doers of the word, and not only hearers."

23. My life will be fruitful, not comfortable. I declare that remaining in Christ produces fruit, according to John 15:5, "bears much fruit."

24. I will finish my race strong. I decree that I run with perseverance, according to Hebrews 12:1, "let us run with perseverance the race that is set before us."

OBEDIENCE ACTIVATION

Confession

Jesus, I repent for comfort addiction, and I surrender my appetites and habits to You.

Action Steps

- Cut one comfort habit today that feeds passivity (scrolling, entertainment, late nights, overeating).
- Choose one hard obedient thing daily for 7 days to retrain

discipline.

- Build a morning routine that puts prayer and Scripture before comfort.
- Fast one thing this week as a direct strike against the flesh.
- Serve someone sacrificially to break the self-centered comfort loop.

Accountability Move

Today, I will tell one trusted believer, "I'm killing comfort addiction. Check on my discipline this week."

CLOSING PRAYER

Father, in Jesus' name, I repent for choosing ease over obedience and comfort over calling. I renounce indulgence, laziness, and every habit that numbs my spirit. Holy Spirit, strengthen my discipline, sharpen my hunger, and teach me to endure and obey. I surrender my schedule, my appetites, and my priorities to Jesus Christ as Lord. I declare that comfort will not kill my purpose, and I will live strong, alert, and obedient. In the name of Jesus, amen.

CHAPTER 15

Break Free From A Critical Spirit & Constant Negativity

If all you do is criticize, you'll never build.

OPENING PRAYER

Father, in Jesus' name, I repent for negativity, complaining, and speaking like a critic instead of a builder. I renounce pride, bitterness, and the habit of tearing down what I'm called to strengthen. Holy Spirit, purify my heart, guard my mouth, and train me to speak life and truth. Amen.

THE ISSUE

A critical spirit feels like discernment, but it usually isn't. It's the reflex to find what's wrong, focus on flaws, assume motives, and highlight failure.

It doesn't just damage relationships. It poisons my own spirit. Because when criticism becomes your language, you stop building and start destroying.

WHY IT'S HAPPENING

- You're using criticism to feel superior instead of staying humble.
- You've been hurt, disappointed, or let down, and cynicism became your shield.
- You've trained yourself to notice problems more than progress.
- You're talking more than you're praying.
- You're reacting out of frustration instead of responding with wisdom.

WHERE IT CAME FROM

A critical spirit often grows out of unresolved pain, pride, insecurity, or disappointment. Sometimes it started when you felt powerless, so your mouth became your weapon.

The root is often bitterness or self-righteousness, but the door stays open through constant negative speech, suspicion, and judgment. And the lie underneath it sounds like this: "If I criticize it, I'm above it." But criticism doesn't elevate you. It corrodes you.

BREAK FREE DECLARATION

I break agreement with a critical spirit, constant negativity, and destructive speech in the name of Jesus Christ.
I reject the lie that tearing down makes me wise or spiritually mature.
Jesus is Lord over my mouth, my thoughts, and my attitude.
I choose humility, encouragement, and truth spoken with love.
I will be a builder, not a critic.

SCRIPTURE-BACKED DECREES

1. My mouth will not be a weapon. I declare that death and life are in the power of the tongue, according to Proverbs 18:21, "Death and life are in the power of the tongue."

2. I will speak words that produce life. I decree that my words will honor God, according to Psalm 19:14, "Let the words of my mouth… be acceptable in your sight."

3. I will not use my mouth to tear down. I declare that corrupt speech must stop, according to Ephesians 4:29, "Let no corrupt speech proceed out of your mouth."

4. My words will build people up. I decree that I speak what gives grace, according to Ephesians 4:29, "that it may give grace to those who hear."

5. I will not live addicted to complaint. I declare that I do all things without complaining, according to Philippians 2:14, "Do all things without complaining and arguing."

6. Negativity will not be my default setting. I decree that I reject arguments and division, according to Philippians 2:14, "without… arguing."

7. I will not judge harshly to feel strong. I declare that the measure I

use will come back to me, according to Matthew 7:2, "For with whatever judgment you judge, you will be judged."

8. I will examine myself before I attack others. I decree that I remove the plank from my own eye, according to Matthew 7:5, "First remove the beam out of your own eye."

9. I will not assume motives. I declare that the Lord judges the heart, according to 1 Corinthians 4:5, "who will both bring to light the hidden things of darkness… and then each man will get his praise from God."

10. Pride will not guide my opinions. I decree that God resists the proud, according to James 4:6, "God resists the proud, but gives grace to the humble."

11. Humility will lead my speech. I declare that I humble myself under God's hand, according to 1 Peter 5:6, "Humble yourselves… under the mighty hand of God."

12. Discernment includes self-control. I decree that God gave me self-control, according to 2 Timothy 1:7, "God didn't give us a spirit of fear, but of power, love, and self-control."

13. I will not repay wrong with harsh words. I declare that I bless instead of striking back, according to 1 Peter 3:9, "but… blessing."

14. Love is my standard, not sarcasm. I decree that love is not rude and not resentful, according to 1 Corinthians 13:5, "doesn't behave itself inappropriately… doesn't take account of evil."

15. I will guard my heart so my mouth stays clean. I declare that I keep my heart with diligence, according to Proverbs 4:23, "Keep your heart with all diligence."

16. My spirit will not be poisoned by bitterness. I decree that bitterness must be removed, according to Ephesians 4:31, "Let all bitterness… be put away from you."

17. I will pursue peace more than being right. I declare that I seek peace and pursue it, according to Psalm 34:14, "Seek peace, and pursue

it."

18. My tone will reflect wisdom. I decree that heavenly wisdom is gentle, according to James 3:17, "peaceable, gentle."

19. My life will produce encouragement, not discouragement. I declare that I strengthen others, according to 1 Thessalonians 5:11, "Encourage one another, and build each other up."

20. I will be quick to listen and slow to speak. I decree that I obey God's order for my mouth, according to James 1:19, "swift to hear, slow to speak."

21. My words will be seasoned with grace. I declare that my speech is gracious, according to Colossians 4:6, "Let your speech always be with grace, seasoned with salt."

22. I will not tear down leaders and call it discernment. I decree that I honor what God appoints, according to Romans 13:7, "Give… honor to whom honor."

23. I will be a peacemaker and a builder. I declare that peacemakers are blessed, according to Matthew 5:9, "Blessed are the peacemakers."

24. I will not criticize what I refuse to contribute to. I decree that faith produces works, according to James 2:17, "faith… is dead in itself."

25. God will purify my speech as I surrender. I declare that the Lord refines me, according to Psalm 141:3, "Set a watch, Yahweh, before my mouth. Keep the door of my lips."

OBEDIENCE ACTIVATION

Confession

Jesus, I repent for negativity and criticism, and I surrender my mouth and attitude to You.

Action Steps

- Catch yourself in the moment and stop negative speech mid-sentence.
- Replace criticism with prayer before you share an opinion.
- Speak 3 decrees daily for 7 days to retrain your mouth.
- Build something this week instead of tearing down what others are doing.
- Encourage one person daily with truth and strength, not flattery.

Accountability Move

Today, I will tell one trusted believer, "I'm breaking negativity. Call me out when I tear down."

CLOSING PRAYER

Father, in Jesus' name, I repent for a critical spirit, negativity, and destructive speech. I renounce pride, bitterness, and the habit of tearing down instead of building. Holy Spirit, guard my mouth, cleanse my heart, and teach me to speak life and truth with love. Make me an encourager, a peacemaker, and a builder in Your Kingdom. I declare that my words will honor You, strengthen others, and reflect maturity. In the name of Jesus, amen.

CHAPTER 16

Break Free From Delayed Obedience & Procrastination
Delayed obedience is still disobedience.

OPENING PRAYER

Father, in Jesus' name, I repent for delay, excuses, and procrastination in areas where You've already spoken. I renounce spiritual hesitation and the habit of pushing obedience into "later." Holy Spirit, give me urgency, courage, and the strength to obey immediately. Amen.

THE ISSUE

Delayed obedience isn't harmless. It's disobedience with better branding. It's when God speaks clearly, but you stall, rationalize, postpone, and negotiate.

You call it waiting, but heaven calls it delay. And the more you delay, the more obedience starts feeling optional instead of required.

WHY IT'S HAPPENING

- You're afraid of what obedience will cost you.
- You want clarity without commitment.
- You're waiting to "feel ready" instead of choosing to obey.
- You've trained yourself to respond slowly to conviction.
- You've turned urgency into convenience and discipline into mood.

WHERE IT CAME FROM

Procrastination often comes from fear: fear of failure, fear of change, fear of discomfort, fear of losing control. Sometimes it comes from laziness, or from being overwhelmed and indecisive.

The root is often self-protection, but the door stays open through excuses, distractions, and partial obedience. And the lie underneath it sounds like this: "Later is safer than now." But later is where purpose dies.

BREAK FREE DECLARATION

I break agreement with delayed obedience, procrastination, and spiritual hesitation in the name of Jesus Christ.
I reject the lie that postponing obedience protects me or gives me more time.
Jesus is Lord over my schedule, my decisions, and my actions.
I choose immediate obedience, decisive faith, and disciplined follow-through.
I will obey when God speaks without delay.

SCRIPTURE-BACKED DECREES

1. God deserves immediate obedience. I declare that to know what is right and not do it is sin, according to James 4:17, "To him therefore who knows to do good and doesn't do it, to him it is sin."

2. I will not treat obedience like an option. I decree that Jesus expects doers, not hearers, according to James 1:22, "But be doers of the word, and not only hearers, deluding your own selves."

3. I will not deceive myself with spiritual listening. I declare that hearing without doing is self-deception, according to James 1:22, "not only hearers, deluding your own selves."

4. God's Word requires action. I decree that obedience is better than sacrifice, according to 1 Samuel 15:22, "To obey is better than sacrifice."

5. I will stop wavering between two opinions. I declare that I follow the Lord fully, according to 1 Kings 18:21, "If Yahweh is God, follow him."

6. Faith is proven by obedience. I decree that faith without works is dead, according to James 2:17, "faith, if it has no works, is dead in itself."

7. I will not waste my life with delay. I declare that I redeem the time, according to Ephesians 5:16, "redeeming the time because the days are evil."

8. Today matters. I decree that I will not harden my heart when God

speaks, according to Hebrews 3:15, "Today if you will hear his voice, don't harden your hearts."

9. I will not ignore conviction. I declare that God corrects those He loves, according to Revelation 3:19, "As many as I love, I reprove and chasten. Be zealous therefore, and repent."

10. I will choose zeal instead of delay. I decree that I obey with urgency, according to Revelation 3:19, "Be zealous therefore."

11. God strengthens me to do what He commands. I declare that God helps me, according to Isaiah 41:10, "I will strengthen you. Yes, I will help you."

12. I will take responsibility for my actions. I decree that each man carries his own load, according to Galatians 6:5, "For each man will bear his own burden."

13. I will not be spiritually sluggish. I declare that God warns against laziness, according to Hebrews 6:12, "that you may not be sluggish."

14. Discipline is part of breakthrough. I decree that I train myself for godliness, according to 1 Timothy 4:7, "train yourself in godliness."

15. God's direction becomes clearer through obedience. I declare that God leads me as I move, according to Proverbs 3:5–6, "In all your ways acknowledge him, and he will make your paths straight."

16. I will not be paralyzed by fear of failure. I decree that God did not give me fear, according to 2 Timothy 1:7, "God didn't give us a spirit of fear."

17. I am called to endurance, not excuses. I declare that perseverance produces maturity, according to James 1:4, "Let perseverance have its perfect work."

18. I will be courageous and obey. I decree that the Lord commands strength and courage, according to Joshua 1:9, "Be strong and courageous... for Yahweh your God is with you."

19. I will not just plan. I will act. I declare that faith requires movement,

according to Proverbs 16:3, "Commit your deeds to Yahweh."

20. God rewards diligence. I decree that diligent hands rule, according to Proverbs 12:24, "The hands of the diligent ones shall rule."

21. I will not be ruled by laziness. I declare that the sluggard craves and gets nothing, according to Proverbs 13:4, "The soul of the sluggard desires, and has nothing."

22. Obedience unlocks fruitfulness. I decree that remaining in Christ produces fruit, according to John 15:5, "He who remains in me... bears much fruit."

23. I will finish what God assigned me. I declare that God completes what He starts, according to Philippians 1:6, "he who began a good work in you will complete it."

24. My life will not be defined by delay. I decree that I press on toward the goal, according to Philippians 3:14, "I press on toward the goal."

OBEDIENCE ACTIVATION

Confession

Jesus, I repent for delayed obedience, and I choose to obey You immediately and fully.

Action Steps

- Write down one thing God told you to do that you've been delaying.
- Take one step today. Small obedience is still obedience.
- Remove one distraction that feeds procrastination and steals focus.
- Speak 3 decrees daily for 7 days to retrain urgency and follow-through.
- Finish one incomplete assignment you've been avoiding and close the loop.

Accountability Move

Today, I will tell one trusted believer, "I'm done delaying. Ask me if I obeyed this week."

CLOSING PRAYER

Father, in Jesus' name, I repent for procrastination, excuses, and delay where You have already spoken. I renounce hesitation, fear, and the habit of pushing obedience into tomorrow. Holy Spirit, strengthen me with urgency, courage, and discipline to obey immediately. I surrender my time, my choices, and my actions to Jesus Christ as Lord. I declare that delayed obedience ends today, and I will walk in decisive faith. In the name of Jesus, amen.

CHAPTER 17

Break Free From Weak Discipline & No Consistency

You don't need more motivation. You need a backbone.

OPENING PRAYER

Father, in Jesus' name, I repent for inconsistency, weak discipline, and starting strong but not finishing well. I renounce excuses, comfort habits, and the mindset that waits for motivation. Holy Spirit, strengthen my will, train my habits, and make me steady in obedience. Amen.

THE ISSUE

Weak discipline looks like good intentions with no follow-through. It's knowing what you should do, but not doing it consistently. It's living in cycles: conviction, effort, drift… then repeat. And without consistency, you don't just lose progress, you lose authority because authority is built through obedience over time.

WHY IT'S HAPPENING

- You've been relying on feelings instead of commitment.
- You've trained yourself to quit when it gets uncomfortable.
- You're consuming too much and producing too little.
- You've been undisciplined with your time, energy, and focus.
- You keep making excuses instead of making changes.

WHERE IT CAME FROM

Weak discipline often starts when you believe consistency is for "stronger people," and not for you. It can come from repeated failure that trained you to expect quitting.

The root is often comfort addiction and self-reliance, but the door stays open through distractions, lack of structure, and unchecked habits. And the lie underneath it sounds like this: "I'll be consistent when I feel ready." But discipline isn't a feeling. It's a decision.

BREAK FREE DECLARATION

I break agreement with weak discipline, inconsistency, and unfinished obedience in the name of Jesus Christ.
I reject the lie that motivation is my solution and discomfort is my enemy.
Jesus is Lord over my habits, my time, and my priorities.
I choose discipline, structure, and steady obedience.
I will become consistent through the power of the Holy Spirit.

SCRIPTURE-BACKED DECREES

1. God calls me to self-control. I declare that self-control is part of spiritual maturity, according to 2 Timothy 1:7, "God didn't give us a spirit of fear, but of power, love, and self-control."

2. Discipline is expected, not optional. I decree that I train myself for godliness, according to 1 Timothy 4:7, "train yourself in godliness."

3. I will not be ruled by my emotions. I declare that I live by faith, not by sight, according to 2 Corinthians 5:7, "for we walk by faith, not by sight."

4. I will not start and quit. I decree that I finish what I begin, according to Ecclesiastes 7:8, "Better is the end of a thing than its beginning."

5. Consistency produces maturity. I declare that perseverance makes me complete, according to James 1:4, "Let perseverance have its perfect work."

6. I will build spiritual endurance. I decree that I run with perseverance, according to Hebrews 12:1, "let us run with perseverance the race that is set before us."

7. I will not live spiritually undisciplined. I declare that a wise man rules his spirit, according to Proverbs 16:32, "He who rules his spirit is better than he who takes a city."

8. Ruling my spirit is strength. I decree that controlling my spirit is greater than brute strength, according to Proverbs 16:32, "better… than he who takes a city."

9. I discipline my body for obedience. I declare that I bring my body into submission, according to 1 Corinthians 9:27, "I bring it into submission."

10. I will not waste my time. I decree that I redeem the time, according to Ephesians 5:16, "redeeming the timebecause the days are evil."

11. Diligence leads to progress. I declare that diligent hands rule, according to Proverbs 12:24, "The hands of the diligent ones shall rule."

12. Laziness will not dominate me. I decree that the sluggard desires and has nothing, according to Proverbs 13:4, "The soul of the sluggard desires, and has nothing."

13. I will not be spiritually sluggish. I declare that God warns against sluggishness, according to Hebrews 6:12, "that you may not be sluggish."

14. I will be steady in obedience. I decree that I am steadfast and immovable, according to 1 Corinthians 15:58, "be steadfast, immovable, always abounding in the Lord's work."

15. God strengthens me for consistency. I declare that the Lord helps me, according to Isaiah 41:10, "I will strengthen you. Yes, I will help you."

16. I will not excuse inconsistency as "personality." I decree that God renews me in discipline, according to Romans 12:2, "be transformed by the renewing of your mind."

17. My faith will show up in my actions. I declare that faith without works is dead, according to James 2:17, "faith… is dead in itself."

18. I will obey the Word, not just hear it. I decree that I am a doer, according to James 1:22, "be doers of the word."

19. Small obedience still counts. I declare that God honors faithfulness in little, according to Luke 16:10, "He who is faithful in a very little is faithful also in much."

20. My habits will align with my calling. I decree that I commit my work to the Lord, according to Proverbs 16:3, "Commit your deeds to Yahweh."

21. I will remain connected to Jesus daily. I declare that remaining in Christ produces fruit, according to John 15:5, "He who remains in me… bears much fruit."

22. My strength comes from Christ, not motivation. I decree that Jesus strengthens me, according to Philippians 4:13, "I can do all things through Christ, who strengthens me."

23. God completes what He starts in me. I declare that He will finish His work, according to Philippians 1:6, "he who began a good work in you will complete it."

24. I will not drift back into old patterns. I decree that I keep watch over my life, according to 1 Peter 5:8, "Be sober and self-controlled. Be watchful."

OBEDIENCE ACTIVATION

Confession

Jesus, I repent for inconsistency, and I surrender my habits and discipline to You.

Action Steps

- Pick one non-negotiable daily habit (prayer, Scripture, exercise, fasting, journaling) and do it for 7 days.
- Remove one weak link that consistently breaks your routine (late nights, scrolling, unplanned mornings).
- Speak 3 decrees daily to reinforce backbone and steady obedience.
- Stop waiting for motivation and obey God in the moment you feel resistance.
- Finish one small task daily to retrain follow-through and consistency.

Accountability Move

Today, I will tell one trusted believer, "I'm building discipline. Check on me daily this week."

CLOSING PRAYER

Father, in Jesus' name, I repent for weak discipline and inconsistency. I renounce excuses, comfort habits, and the mindset that waits for motivation. Holy Spirit, strengthen my spine, train my habits, and make me steady in obedience. I surrender my time, my routines, and my priorities to Jesus Christ as Lord. I declare that I will live disciplined, consistent, and fruitful for Your Kingdom. In the name of Jesus, amen.

CHAPTER 18

Break Free From Laziness & Sloth

Sloth isn't rest. It's resistance to responsibility.

OPENING PRAYER

Father, in Jesus' name, I repent for laziness, excuses, and avoiding responsibility. I renounce sloth, procrastination, and the habits that keep me unproductive and spiritually dull. Holy Spirit, strengthen my discipline, renew my energy, and train me to work with purpose. Amen.

THE ISSUE

Sloth is not rest.

Rest is recovery with intention. Sloth is avoidance with excuses. It's the habit of delaying responsibility, resisting structure, and choosing ease over stewardship. And if you keep feeding sloth, your life won't just stay unproductive. It will stay powerless.

WHY IT'S HAPPENING

- You're choosing comfort over calling.
- You're addicted to escape and calling it "self-care."
- You're avoiding effort because you don't want to face failure.
- You're letting distraction steal your focus and energy.
- You're waiting to "feel like it" instead of choosing discipline.

WHERE IT CAME FROM

Laziness often grows where purpose is unclear and responsibility feels heavy. Sometimes sloth is rooted in fear. Fear of effort, fear of failure, fear of discomfort. Other times it comes from indulgence and undisciplined habits that trained you to choose easy.

The root is resistance, but the door stays open through excuses, delayed obedience, and comfort addiction. And the lie underneath it sounds like this:

"It can wait, and I'll still be fine." But sloth always collects interest.

BREAK FREE DECLARATION

I break agreement with laziness, sloth, and avoidance in the name of Jesus Christ.
I reject the lie that comfort is harmless and responsibility is optional.
Jesus is Lord over my energy, my habits, and my stewardship.
I choose diligence, discipline, and purposeful work.
I will build what God assigned me, and I will not waste my life.

SCRIPTURE-BACKED DECREES

1. God calls me to diligence, not sloth. I declare that lazy hands lead to poverty, according to Proverbs 10:4, "He becomes poor who works with a lazy hand."

2. My work will be marked by diligence. I decree that the hand of the diligent makes rich, according to Proverbs 10:4, "but the hand of the diligent brings wealth."

3. Laziness will not rule my future. I declare that the sluggard desires and has nothing, according to Proverbs 13:4, "The soul of the sluggard desires, and has nothing."

4. God rewards diligent effort. I decree that the diligent soul is made rich, according to Proverbs 13:4, "but the desire of the diligent shall be fully satisfied."

5. Sloth leads to loss. I declare that a little sleep and folding hands brings poverty, according to Proverbs 6:10–11, "A little sleep… so your poverty will come."

6. My life will not drift into lack. I decree that want will not overtake me, according to Proverbs 6:11, "and your want as an armed man."

7. I will not make excuses to avoid responsibility. I declare that excuses are a trap, according to Proverbs 22:13, "The sluggard says, 'There is a lion outside!'"

8. God strengthens me to work faithfully. I decree that the Lord

strengthens my hands, according to Isaiah 41:10, "I will strengthen you. Yes, I will help you."

9. I will work as unto the Lord. I declare that my work is worship, according to Colossians 3:23, "Whatever you do, work heartily, as for the Lord."

10. I will not live careless with time. I decree that I redeem the time, according to Ephesians 5:16, "redeeming the timebecause the days are evil."

11. My life will produce fruit, not excuses. I declare that remaining in Christ produces fruit, according to John 15:5, "He who remains in me… bears much fruit."

12. I will not be spiritually sluggish. I decree that God warns against sluggishness, according to Hebrews 6:12, "that you may not be sluggish."

13. I will be steadfast in responsibility. I declare that I am immovable and abounding, according to 1 Corinthians 15:58, "always abounding in the Lord's work."

14. My strength grows through discipline. I decree that I train myself for godliness, according to 1 Timothy 4:7, "train yourself in godliness."

15. I will not be ruled by the flesh. I declare that the flesh leads to death, according to Romans 8:13, "if you live after the flesh, you must die."

16. The Spirit empowers productive living. I decree that I put to death lazy patterns by the Spirit, according to Romans 8:13, "but if by the Spirit you put to death the deeds of the body, you will live."

17. My mind will be renewed in discipline. I declare that I will be transformed, according to Romans 12:2, "be transformed by the renewing of your mind."

18. I will not waste my assignment. I decree that God prepared good works for me, according to Ephesians 2:10, "created… for good works… that we should walk in them."

19. I will not despise small beginnings. I declare that God honors progress, according to Zechariah 4:10, "For who despises the day of small things?"

20. Faith requires action, not intentions. I decree that faith without works is dead, according to James 2:17, "faith… is dead in itself."

21. I will not delay what God told me to do. I declare that delayed obedience is sin, according to James 4:17, "and doesn't do it, to him it is sin."

22. God blesses faithfulness in little. I decree that faithfulness in small things matters, according to Luke 16:10, "He who is faithful in a very little is faithful also in much."

23. I will not grow weary in doing good. I declare that I will reap if I don't give up, according to Galatians 6:9, "Let us not be weary in doing good… we will reap."

24. My life will be disciplined and alert. I decree that I stay watchful, according to 1 Peter 5:8, "Be sober and self-controlled. Be watchful."

OBEDIENCE ACTIVATION

Confession

Jesus, I repent for laziness, and I choose diligence and responsibility under Your lordship.

Action Steps

- Do one hard thing today that you've been avoiding. No delay.
- Create a simple daily structure (wake time, prayer time, work blocks) and follow it for 7 days.
- Remove one lazy trigger (late nights, endless scrolling, comfort habits that steal energy).
- Speak 3 decrees daily to retrain discipline and responsibility.
- Finish one task fully each day instead of starting many and completing none.

Accountability Move

Today, I will tell one trusted believer, "I'm breaking laziness. Ask me what I built this week."

CLOSING PRAYER

Father, in Jesus' name, I repent for sloth, avoidance, and resisting responsibility. I renounce excuses, comfort addiction, and the patterns that keep me unproductive and weak. Holy Spirit, strengthen my discipline, renew my energy, and train me to work with purpose. I surrender my time, my habits, and my stewardship to Jesus Christ as Lord. I declare that laziness ends here, and diligence will mark my life.
In the name of Jesus, amen.

CHAPTER 19

Break Free From Isolation

You called it "peace." God calls it hiding.

OPENING PRAYER

Father, in Jesus' name, I repent for hiding, withdrawing, and choosing isolation when You called me to community. I renounce fear, pride, shame, and self-protection that keeps me disconnected. Holy Spirit, heal what drove me into hiding and lead me back into healthy fellowship. Amen.

THE ISSUE

Isolation doesn't always look like loneliness. Sometimes it looks like "I'm just protecting my peace." But when you cut yourself off from people, accountability, and real fellowship, you don't become stronger. You become vulnerable. Because isolation is where temptation grows, lies get louder, and wounds stay untreated.

WHY IT'S HAPPENING

- You're tired of being hurt, so you stopped trusting.
- You're carrying shame, so you avoid being known.
- You've been disappointed by people, so you withdrew.
- You're afraid of correction, accountability, or exposure.
- You've convinced yourself you're "better alone," but you're just unprotected.

WHERE IT CAME FROM

Isolation often starts after betrayal, rejection, church hurt, conflict, or repeated disappointment. Sometimes it begins when you get overwhelmed and choose withdrawal as a coping mechanism.

The root can be pain or pride, but the door stays open through avoidance, secrecy, and unhealed wounds. And the lie underneath it sounds like this: "If I stay alone, I can't get hurt." But the truth is: if you stay alone, you also can't get healed.

BREAK FREE DECLARATION

I break agreement with isolation, hiding, and disconnection in the name of
Jesus Christ.
I reject the lie that cutting myself off is peace or that solitude will heal what
only truth can heal.
Jesus is Lord over my relationships, my trust, and my healing process.
I choose healthy community, accountability, and fellowship.
I will come into the light and walk in freedom.

SCRIPTURE-BACKED DECREES

1. God did not create me to live disconnected. I declare that it is not good for man to be alone, according to Genesis 2:18, "It is not good for the man to be alone."

2. Isolation opens a door to foolishness. I decree that isolation leads to selfish desire, according to Proverbs 18:1, "A man who isolates himself pursues selfishness."

3. Isolation fights against wisdom. I declare that separating myself resists sound judgment, according to Proverbs 18:1, "and defies all sound judgment."

4. God designed the body to function together. I decree that believers need each other, according to 1 Corinthians 12:21, "The eye can't tell the hand, 'I have no need for you.'"

5. I am not called to do life alone. I declare that God placed members in the body by His design, according to 1 Corinthians 12:18, "God has set the members… in the body, just as he desired."

6. Strength is multiplied in community. I decree that two are better than one, according to Ecclesiastes 4:9, "Two are better than one because they have a good reward for their labor."

7. I will not fall alone and stay down. I declare that God uses people to lift me, according to Ecclesiastes 4:10, "If they fall, the one will lift up his fellow."

8. Isolation makes me vulnerable. I decree that a cord of three strands is not quickly broken, according to Ecclesiastes 4:12, "A threefold cord is not quickly broken."

9. Confession breaks bondage. I declare that confession and prayer bring healing, according to James 5:16, "Confess your offenses to one another… that you may be healed."

10. God heals through accountability and prayer. I decree that prayer is effective, according to James 5:16, "The effective, fervent prayer of a righteous man avails much."

11. Walking in the light produces fellowship. I declare that walking in truth creates unity, according to 1 John 1:7, "if we walk in the light… we have fellowship with one another."

12. The blood of Jesus cleanses me. I decree that Jesus cleanses me as I walk in the light, according to 1 John 1:7, "the blood of Jesus Christ… cleanses us from all sin."

13. I will not neglect gathering with believers. I declare that fellowship is commanded, according to Hebrews 10:25, "not forsaking our own assembling together."

14. Community strengthens me toward love and obedience. I decree that believers stir one another to good works, according to Hebrews 10:24, "consider how to provoke one another to love and good works."

15. God comforts me so I can connect again. I declare that God comforts and restores, according to 2 Corinthians 1:3–4, "the Father of mercies and God of all comfort."

16. I am not meant to carry burdens alone. I decree that burdens are shared, according to Galatians 6:2, "Bear one another's burdens."

17. Isolation is not humility. I declare that pride isolates, according to Proverbs 16:18, "Pride goes before destruction."

18. God gives grace to the humble. I decree that humility opens the door to help, according to James 4:6, "God resists the proud, but gives grace to the humble."

19. Shame will not keep me hidden. I declare that I confess and receive cleansing, according to 1 John 1:9, "to cleanse us from all unrighteousness."

20. God restores my soul, not just my mood. I decree that the Lord restores me, according to Psalm 23:3, "He restores my soul."

21. The enemy targets isolated believers. I declare that I stay watchful, according to 1 Peter 5:8, "Be sober and self-controlled. Be watchful."

22. My strength grows through connection. I decree that encouragement builds faith, according to 1 Thessalonians 5:11, "Encourage one another, and build each other up."

23. I will pursue peace the right way. I declare that I seek peace and pursue it, according to Psalm 34:14, "Seek peace, and pursue it."

24. God leads me into family, not hiding. I decree that God sets the lonely in families, according to Psalm 68:6, "God sets the lonely in families."

OBEDIENCE ACTIVATION

Confession

Jesus, I repent for hiding in isolation, and I choose to walk in the light with Your people.

Action Steps

- Reach out today to one trusted believer and schedule a real conversation.
- Join a consistent community (local church, men's group, Bible study) and commit for 30 days.
- Confess one struggle you've been hiding and let prayer break it.
- Speak 3 decrees daily for 7 days to break the hiding mindset.
- Stop calling isolation "peace" and start practicing connection as obedience.

Accountability Move

Today, I will message one trusted believer, "I've been isolating. Can you walk with me and pray with me?"

CLOSING PRAYER

Father, in Jesus' name, I repent for hiding, withdrawing, and choosing isolation instead of fellowship. I renounce shame, fear, pride, and self-protection that keeps me disconnected. Holy Spirit, heal my heart, restore trust, and lead me into healthy community and accountability. I surrender my relationships and my healing process to Jesus Christ as Lord. I declare that I will walk in the light, live in fellowship, and break free from isolation. In the name of Jesus, amen.

CHAPTER 20

Break Free From Control & Micromanaging

Trying to control everything is a sign you don't trust God.

OPENING PRAYER

Father, in Jesus' name, I repent for trying to control outcomes, people, and situations instead of trusting You. I renounce anxiety-driven control, micromanaging, and the fear that fuels it. Holy Spirit, teach me surrender, strengthen my trust, and lead me into peace-filled obedience. Amen.

THE ISSUE

Control feels like wisdom, but it's often fear in disguise. Micromanaging is what happens when you believe everything depends on you. It drains your peace, strains your relationships, and keeps your heart clenched instead of surrendered. Because when you must control everything, you're not trusting God. You're replacing Him.

WHY IT'S HAPPENING

- You're afraid of uncertainty, so you try to manage everything.
- You've been disappointed before, so you control to prevent pain.
- You believe outcomes depend on my perfection, not God's providence.
- You confuse responsibility with control.
- You have a hard time letting people fail, learn, or grow.

WHERE IT CAME FROM

Control often develops where trust was broken: unstable childhood, unpredictable leadership, betrayal, trauma, or constant disappointment. It can also come from pride: the belief that you know best and must manage every detail.

The root is fear and self-reliance, but the door stays open through anxiety, micromanaging, and refusing surrender. And the lie underneath it sounds like this: "If I don't control it, it will fall apart." But God has never asked you to be sovereign… only obedient.

BREAK FREE DECLARATION

I break agreement with control, micromanaging, and anxiety-driven striving in the name of Jesus Christ.
I reject the lie that I must manage everything to be safe or successful.
Jesus is Lord over my outcomes, my plans, and my relationships.
I choose trust, surrender, and Spirit-led wisdom.
I will do my part faithfully and leave the results in God's hands.

SCRIPTURE-BACKED DECREES

1. Trust is my assignment, not control. I declare that I trust in Yahweh with all my heart, according to Proverbs 3:5, "Trust in Yahweh with all your heart, and don't lean on your own understanding."

2. I will not lean on my own understanding. I decree that I submit my perspective to God, according to Proverbs 3:5, "don't lean on your own understanding."

3. God directs my path when I surrender. I declare that the Lord makes my paths straight, according to Proverbs 3:6, "In all your ways acknowledge him, and he will make your paths straight."

4. Worry and control are not the same as wisdom. I decree that anxiety has no authority over me, according to Philippians 4:6, "In nothing be anxious."

5. Prayer replaces control with peace. I declare that I bring my requests to God, according to Philippians 4:6, "by prayer… let your requests be made known to God."

6. God's peace guards me when I surrender. I decree that God's peace guards my heart, according to Philippians 4:7, "The peace of God… will guard your hearts and your thoughts."

7. God is the one holding my life together. I declare that God works all things for good, according to Romans 8:28, "all things work together for good."

8. I am not sovereign. God is. I decree that the Lord is God and there is no other, according to Isaiah 45:5, "I am Yahweh, and there is no one else."

9. My job is faithfulness, not domination. I declare that God rewards faithful stewardship, according to Luke 16:10, "He who is faithful in a very little is faithful also in much."

10. I will commit my plans to God. I decree that I commit my work to Yahweh, according to Proverbs 16:3, "Commit your deeds to Yahweh."

11. God establishes what I surrender. I declare that my plans are established under God, according to Proverbs 16:3, "and your plans shall succeed."

12. I release what I cannot control. I decree that I cast my cares on God, according to 1 Peter 5:7, "casting all your worries on him because he cares for you."

13. God cares for me deeply. I declare that the Lord cares for me, according to 1 Peter 5:7, "because he cares for you."

14. I will not be driven by fear. I decree that God gave me self-control, according to 2 Timothy 1:7, "God didn't give us a spirit of fear."

15. The Holy Spirit leads me, not panic. I declare that I am led by the Spirit of God, according to Romans 8:14, "as many as are led by the Spirit of God."

16. God gives wisdom when I ask. I decree that God gives wisdom generously, according to James 1:5, "let him ask of God… and it will be given to him."

17. I can rest because God never sleeps. I declare that God watches over me, according to Psalm 121:4, "he who keeps Israel will neither slumber nor sleep."

18. The Lord fights battles I can't control. I decree that God fights for me, according to Exodus 14:14, "Yahweh will fight for you, and you shall be still."

19. I choose obedience over over-management. I declare that obedience is better than sacrifice, according to 1 Samuel 15:22, "To obey is

better than sacrifice."

20. Humility breaks the need to control. I decree that God gives grace to the humble, according to James 4:6, "God resists the proud, but gives grace to the humble."

21. I will surrender outcomes to the Lord. I declare that my life belongs to God, according to Romans 14:8, "if we live, we live to the Lord."

22. I will build with faith, not striving. I decree that apart from Christ I can do nothing, according to John 15:5, "Apart from me you can do nothing."

23. God strengthens me to do my part well. I declare that God helps me, according to Isaiah 41:10, "I will strengthen you. Yes, I will help you."

24. I will not control people through pressure. I decree that my words will be gracious, according to Colossians 4:6, "Let your speech always be with grace."

25. God completes what He starts. I declare that God finishes His work in me, according to Philippians 1:6, "he who began a good work in you will complete it."

OBEDIENCE ACTIVATION

Confession

Jesus, I repent for control and micromanaging, and I surrender outcomes and people into Your hands.

Action Steps

- Identify one area you've been over-controlling and release it to God in prayer today.
- Replace control with prayer every time anxiety rises.
- Delegate one thing instead of gripping it, and let others grow.
- Speak 3 decrees daily for 7 days to retrain trust and surrender.
- Do your part faithfully and stop obsessing over what you can't manage.

Accountability Move

Today, I will tell one trusted believer, "I'm surrendering control. Ask me if I'm trusting God this week."

CLOSING PRAYER

Father, in Jesus' name, I repent for anxiety-driven control and trying to manage everything myself. I renounce micromanaging, fear, and self-reliance that has stolen my peace. Holy Spirit, teach me surrender, strengthen my trust, and lead me into Spirit-led wisdom. I surrender my plans, my outcomes, and my relationships to Jesus Christ as Lord. I declare that I will trust God, walk in peace, and live free from control. In the name of Jesus, amen.

CHAPTER 21

Break Free From Pornography & Sexual Sin

Private compromise always becomes public weakness.

OPENING PRAYER

Father, in Jesus' name, I repent for pornography, sexual sin, and every private compromise I've justified or hidden. I renounce lust, impurity, and every agreement with darkness and secrecy. Holy Spirit, cleanse me, strengthen me, and lead me into purity, freedom, and disciplined obedience. Amen.

THE ISSUE

Pornography and sexual sin don't stay private. What you feed in secret always shapes what you carry in public. It dulls conviction, contaminates intimacy, fuels shame, and fractures spiritual authority. Because when you compromise in private, you don't just lose purity. You lose power.

WHY IT'S HAPPENING

- You've used lust as comfort instead of dealing with pain.
- You've trained your brain to chase quick pleasure instead of real intimacy.
- You've kept it secret, and secrecy keeps it strong.
- You've tolerated temptation instead of fleeing it.
- You've believed you can manage sin without killing it.

WHERE IT CAME FROM

Pornography addiction is rarely just about sex. It's often about escape. It grows in loneliness, stress, rejection, boredom, unresolved wounds, and lack of discipline. The root is lust mixed with comfort-seeking, but the door stays open through secrecy, easy access, and unchecked triggers. And the lie underneath it sounds like this: "It's private, so it's not deadly." But private compromise always becomes public weakness because sin never stays contained.

BREAK FREE DECLARATION

I break agreement with pornography, lust, and sexual sin in the name of
Jesus Christ.
I reject the lie that compromise is harmless and secrecy is safe.
Jesus is Lord over my body, my eyes, my thoughts, and my desires.
I choose purity, holiness, and self-control through the power of the Holy
Spirit.
I will not feed darkness in private and expect strength in public.

SCRIPTURE-BACKED DECREES

1. I am called to purity, not compromise. I declare that God's will is
   my sanctification, according to 1 Thessalonians 4:3, "For this is the
   will of God: your sanctification, that you abstain from sexual
   immorality."

2. I will abstain from sexual immorality. I decree that I refuse sexual
   sin, according to 1 Thessalonians 4:3, "that you abstain from sexual
   immorality."

3. Self-control is required for holiness. I declare that I possess my
   body in holiness, according to 1 Thessalonians 4:4, "that each one
   of you know how to possess himself of his own vessel in
   sanctification and honor."

4. I will honor God with my body. I decree that my body belongs to
   the Lord, according to 1 Corinthians 6:19–20, "your body is a
   temple of the Holy Spirit… For you were bought with a price."

5. My eyes will not be a doorway to sin. I declare that I set no vile
   thing before my eyes, according to Psalm 101:3, "I will set no vile
   thing before my eyes."

6. Lust will not rule my mind. I decree that I take my thoughts captive,
   according to 2 Corinthians 10:5, "bringing every thought into
   captivity to the obedience of Christ."

7. I will flee temptation, not flirt with it. I declare that I flee sexual
   immorality, according to 1 Corinthians 6:18, "Flee sexual
   immorality."

8. Sin does not own me. I decree that sin will not have dominion over me, according to Romans 6:14, "For sin will not have dominion over you."

9. God provides an escape route. I declare that God makes a way of escape, according to 1 Corinthians 10:13, "God is faithful... will also make the way of escape."

10. I will walk in the light, not secrecy. I decree that walking in the light brings cleansing, according to 1 John 1:7, "if we walk in the light... the blood of Jesus Christ... cleanses us."

11. Confession breaks the power of hidden sin. I declare that confession leads to forgiveness and cleansing, according to 1 John 1:9, "If we confess our sins... to cleanse us from all unrighteousness."

12. I am not condemned. I am called to repent. I decree that there is no condemnation in Christ, according to Romans 8:1, "There is therefore now no condemnation."

13. Grace trains me to say no to ungodliness. I declare that grace teaches discipline, according to Titus 2:11–12, "teaching us that... we should live soberly, righteously, and godly."

14. My life will not be mastered by lust. I decree that I will not be brought under the power of anything, according to 1 Corinthians 6:12, "I will not be brought under the power of any."

15. Purity is a command, not a suggestion. I declare that God calls me to be holy, according to 1 Peter 1:15–16, "Be holy; for I am holy."

16. I will not make provision for the flesh. I decree that I starve sinful cravings, according to Romans 13:14, "make no provision for the flesh."

17. My body is for the Lord. I declare that the body is not for sexual immorality, according to 1 Corinthians 6:13, "The body is not for sexual immorality, but for the Lord."

18. I will pursue righteousness with discipline. I decree that I pursue righteousness, faith, love, and peace, according to 2 Timothy 2:22, "Flee youthful lusts, but pursue righteousness."

19. God renews my desires over time. I declare that I am transformed

by renewing my mind, according to Romans 12:2, "be transformed by the renewing of your mind."

20. The Holy Spirit empowers purity. I decree that I walk by the Spirit and won't fulfill lust, according to Galatians 5:16, "Walk by the Spirit, and you won't fulfill the lust of the flesh."

21. God strengthens me when I'm weak. I declare that God strengthens me, according to Isaiah 41:10, "I will strengthen you. Yes, I will help you."

22. I choose covenant faithfulness. I decree that marriage is honorable and the sexually immoral are judged, according to Hebrews 13:4, "Let marriage be held in honor… for God will judge the sexually immoral."

23. I will not be deceived by the short-term payoff. I declare that sin leads to death, according to James 1:14–15, "lust… gives birth to sin… and sin… brings forth death."

24. My freedom will be maintained through obedience. I decree that I resist the devil, according to James 4:7, "Resist the devil, and he will flee from you."

25. I will live clean in secret and strong in public. I declare that God sees in secret and rewards obedience, according to Matthew 6:6, "your Father who sees in secret will reward you."

OBEDIENCE ACTIVATION

Confession

Jesus, I repent for pornography and sexual sin, and I surrender my body, mind, and desires to You.

Action Steps

- Confess it to God and bring it into the light with one trusted believer today.
- Cut access immediately (filters, accountability software, deleting triggers, removing apps).

- Flee triggers. Don't negotiate. Leave the room, shut it down, change environments.
- Speak 3 decrees daily for 30 days to retrain your mind and rebuild spiritual backbone.
- Replace lust with discipline: prayer, Scripture, exercise, sleep, and structure.

Accountability Move

Today, I will tell one trusted believer, "I'm breaking sexual sin. Hold me accountable and pray with me."

CLOSING PRAYER

Father, in Jesus' name, I repent for lust, pornography, and sexual compromise. I renounce secrecy, shame, and every agreement with impurity. Holy Spirit, cleanse me, strengthen my self-control, and train me to flee temptation and walk in holiness. I surrender my eyes, thoughts, body, and desires to Jesus Christ as Lord. I declare that private compromise ends today, and purity will mark my life. In the name of Jesus, amen.

CHAPTER 22

Break Free From Lust & Fantasy

Your body doesn't have to move for sin to grow.

OPENING PRAYER

Father, in Jesus' name, I repent for lust, fantasy, and allowing my mind to entertain what my spirit knows is wrong. I renounce impurity, secret desire, and every thought pattern that feeds sin in private. Holy Spirit, cleanse my mind, retrain my desires, and lead me into purity and self-control. Amen.

THE ISSUE

Lust is not just what you do. It's what you feed. Fantasy is what happens when you let sin grow in imagination before it ever grows in action.

Your body doesn't have to move for bondage to deepen. Your mind is enough. Because what you rehearse in secret eventually becomes what you crave in public.

WHY IT'S HAPPENING

- You've allowed lustful thoughts to linger instead of cutting them off.
- You're feeding your mind with images, content, and entertainment that stirs temptation.
- You've confused attraction with indulgence.
- You're using fantasy as an escape from stress, loneliness, or insecurity.
- You're letting desire lead instead of the Spirit.

WHERE IT CAME FROM

Lust and fantasy often grow from unmet needs, loneliness, boredom, insecurity, or deep disappointment. They can also be the result of years of exposure. Where your mind has been trained to sexualize everything.

The root is impurity mixed with self-comfort, but the door stays open through unguarded eyes, unfiltered entertainment, and unchallenged thoughts. And the lie underneath it sounds like this: "It's only in my head, so it doesn't matter." But Jesus makes it clear that sin starts in the heart.

BREAK FREE DECLARATION

I break agreement with lust, fantasy, and impurity in the name of Jesus Christ.
I reject the lie that mental compromise is harmless or that secret desire is not sin.
Jesus is Lord over my thoughts, my eyes, and my desires.
I choose a clean mind, a disciplined imagination, and purity through the Holy Spirit.
I will not feed lust in my mind and expect freedom in my life.

SCRIPTURE-BACKED DECREES

1. Lust is not harmless. It is sin in the heart. I declare that Jesus exposes lust as adultery of the heart, according to Matthew 5:28, "Everyone who looks at a woman to lust after her has committed adultery with her already in his heart."

2. I will cut off lust at the thought level. I decree that I do not entertain it, according to Matthew 5:29, "If your right eye causes you to stumble, pluck it out."

3. I will remove what feeds temptation. I declare that removing the source is wisdom, according to Matthew 5:29, "it is more profitable… than for your whole body to be cast into Gehenna."

4. My eyes will not be a doorway to fantasy. I decree that I set no vile thing before my eyes, according to Psalm 101:3, "I will set no vile thing before my eyes."

5. My mind will not be a playground for impurity. I declare that I take thoughts captive, according to 2 Corinthians 10:5, "bringing every thought into captivity to the obedience of Christ."

6. I will not let sinful thoughts roam free. I decree that my thoughts submit to Jesus, according to 2 Corinthians 10:5, "to the obedience

of Christ."

7. I will not make provision for the flesh. I declare that I starve lust, according to Romans 13:14, "make no provision for the flesh, for its lusts."

8. The Holy Spirit empowers purity. I decree that I walk by the Spirit, according to Galatians 5:16, "Walk by the Spirit, and you won't fulfill the lust of the flesh."

9. My mind will be renewed, not corrupted. I declare that I am transformed by renewing my mind, according to Romans 12:2, "be transformed by the renewing of your mind."

10. God's will is my sanctification. I decree that I abstain from sexual immorality, according to 1 Thessalonians 4:3, "that you abstain from sexual immorality."

11. My thoughts will be disciplined toward what is pure. I declare that I think on what is pure, according to Philippians 4:8, "whatever things are pure… think about these things."

12. I will not be mastered by desire. I decree that I will not be brought under the power of anything, according to 1 Corinthians 6:12, "I will not be brought under the power of any."

13. My body belongs to the Lord. I declare that my body is a temple of the Holy Spirit, according to 1 Corinthians 6:19, "your body is a temple of the Holy Spirit."

14. I am bought with a price. I decree that I glorify God in my body, according to 1 Corinthians 6:20, "glorify God in your body."

15. I will flee lust, not manage it. I declare that I flee youthful lusts, according to 2 Timothy 2:22, "Flee youthful lusts."

16. I will pursue righteousness instead of fantasy. I decree that I pursue righteousness and peace, according to 2 Timothy 2:22, "but pursue righteousness, faith, love, and peace."

17. Sin starts with desire, so I cut it off early. I declare that lust gives birth to sin, according to James 1:14–15, "each one is tempted… by his own lust."

18. I refuse the path that leads to death. I decree that sin brings death, according to James 1:15, "sin… brings forth death."

19. Confession brings cleansing. I declare that God cleanses me when I confess, according to 1 John 1:9, "to cleanse us from all unrighteousness."

20. Walking in the light breaks the power of fantasy. I decree that the blood of Jesus cleanses me, according to 1 John 1:7, "the blood of Jesus Christ… cleanses us from all sin."

21. My heart will stay guarded. I declare that guarding my heart protects my life, according to Proverbs 4:23, "Keep your heart with all diligence."

22. God strengthens me when temptation hits. I decree that God provides a way out, according to 1 Corinthians 10:13, "will also make the way of escape."

23. Purity is the standard God commands. I declare that God calls me to be holy, according to 1 Peter 1:15–16, "Be holy; for I am holy."

24. My secret life will be clean and strong. I decree that God sees in secret, according to Matthew 6:6, "your Father who sees in secret will reward you."

OBEDIENCE ACTIVATION

Confession

Jesus, I repent for lust and fantasy, and I surrender my mind, eyes, and imagination to You.

Action Steps

- Cut off the thought early the moment it enters. No delay, no flirting.
- Remove what feeds fantasy (shows, accounts, images, music, private scrolling).
- Replace temptation immediately with prayer and Scripture out loud.
- Speak 3 decrees daily for 30 days to retrain your mind toward purity.

- Bring it into the light with accountability if this has become a pattern.

Accountability Move

Today, I will tell one trusted believer, "I'm fighting lust at the thought level. Ask me how my mind is doing."

CLOSING PRAYER

Father, in Jesus' name, I repent for lustful thoughts, fantasies, and hidden desire. I renounce impurity, mental compromise, and everything that feeds temptation. Holy Spirit, cleanse my mind, strengthen my self-control, and train me to take every thought captive. I surrender my imagination and desires to Jesus Christ as Lord. I declare that lust will not grow in secret, and purity will mark my mind and life. In the name of Jesus, amen.

CHAPTER 23

Break Free From Drug Use & Substance Reliance

If you can't stop, you're not in control.

OPENING PRAYER

Father, in Jesus' name, I repent for relying on substances for relief, escape, or control. I renounce addiction, dependence, and every false comfort I've turned to instead of You. Holy Spirit, strengthen me, deliver me, and lead me into sobriety, clarity, and freedom. Amen.

THE ISSUE

Substance reliance is what happens when you need something created to function instead of depending on the Creator. It starts as a habit, but it becomes a master. It dulls conviction, weakens discipline, and can wreck relationships, finances, purpose, and spiritual authority. Because if you can't stop, you're not in control, and God never called you to live mastered by anything.

WHY IT'S HAPPENING

- You're using substances to numb pain instead of healing it.
- You're chasing relief from stress, anxiety, loneliness, or trauma.
- You've built a coping pattern that feels necessary to function.
- You've been surrounded by environments that normalize dependence.
- You've been hiding it, and secrecy keeps it strong.

WHERE IT CAME FROM

Drug use and substance reliance often start as self-medication. It can be rooted in anxiety, depression, trauma, rejection, exhaustion, or deep insecurity.

The root is pain and escape, but the door stays open through repeated use, tolerance, and a refusal to confront the real need underneath. And the lie underneath it sounds like this: "This is the only way I can cope." But what feels like coping is often chains tightening slowly.

BREAK FREE DECLARATION

I break agreement with addiction, substance reliance, and every counterfeit comfort in the name of Jesus Christ.
I reject the lie that I need substances to survive, relax, or function.
Jesus is Lord over my body, mind, emotions, and appetite.
I choose sobriety, self-control, and Spirit-empowered freedom.
I will not be mastered by anything but Christ.

SCRIPTURE-BACKED DECREES

1. I will not be mastered by anything. I declare that I refuse bondage, according to 1 Corinthians 6:12, "All things are lawful for me, but I will not be brought under the power of any."

2. God calls me to self-control. I decree that self-control is part of the Spirit's work in me, according to Galatians 5:22–23, "the fruit of the Spirit is… self-control."

3. Sobriety is commanded, not optional. I declare that I will stay sober and watchful, according to 1 Peter 5:8, "Be sober and self-controlled. Be watchful."

4. Addiction is not my identity. I decree that I am not enslaved to sin, according to Romans 6:6, "that the body of sin might be done away with, that we should no longer be in bondage to sin."

5. Sin does not have dominion over me. I declare that sin will not rule me, according to Romans 6:14, "For sin will not have dominion over you."

6. My body belongs to the Lord. I decree that my body is God's temple, according to 1 Corinthians 6:19, "your body is a temple of the Holy Spirit."

7. I will honor God with my body. I declare that I glorify God physically, according to 1 Corinthians 6:20, "glorify God in your body."

8. God strengthens me when cravings hit. I decree that God provides an escape route, according to 1 Corinthians 10:13, "will also make the way of escape."

9. I will resist temptation and stand. I declare that the devil flees when I resist, according to James 4:7, "Resist the devil, and he will flee from you."

10. Grace trains me to say no. I decree that God's grace teaches discipline, according to Titus 2:11–12, "teaching us that… we should live soberly."

11. God did not give me bondage. I declare that God gives me self-control and power, according to 2 Timothy 1:7, "God didn't give us a spirit of fear… but… self-control."

12. Peace is found in prayer, not chemicals. I decree that I bring my needs to God, according to Philippians 4:6, "by prayer… let your requests be made known to God."

13. God's peace guards my mind. I declare that peace will guard me, according to Philippians 4:7, "will guard your hearts and your thoughts."

14. I will walk in the light and get help. I decree that confession breaks secrecy, according to 1 John 1:7, "if we walk in the light… we have fellowship."

15. God cleanses me when I confess. I declare that God forgives and cleanses me, according to 1 John 1:9, "to cleanse us from all unrighteousness."

16. I choose a renewed mind. I decree that I am transformed by renewing my mind, according to Romans 12:2, "be transformed by the renewing of your mind."

17. My strength comes from Christ. I declare that Jesus strengthens me, according to Philippians 4:13, "I can do all things through Christ, who strengthens me."

18. God is close to the broken and overwhelmed. I decree that the Lord is near, according to Psalm 34:18, "Yahweh is near to those who have a broken heart."

19. God heals what drove me to escape. I declare that God heals my wounds, according to Psalm 147:3, "He heals the brokenhearted."

20. Community is part of freedom. I decree that I bear burdens with others, according to Galatians 6:2, "Bear one another's burdens."

21. I will not be spiritually asleep. I declare that it's time to wake up, according to Romans 13:11, "awake out of sleep."

22. God renews my strength over time. I decree that the Lord renews my strength, according to Isaiah 40:31, "will renew their strength."

23. Obedience is my new pattern. I declare that I am a doer of the Word, according to James 1:22, "be doers of the word."

24. Freedom is my inheritance in Christ. I decree that where the Spirit is, there is liberty, according to 2 Corinthians 3:17, "where the Spirit of the Lord is, there is liberty."

25. I will live sober, clear, and useful for God's purpose. I declare that I walk as children of light, according to Ephesians 5:8, "walk as children of light."

OBEDIENCE ACTIVATION

Confession

Jesus, I repent for substance reliance, and I surrender my body and cravings to You for freedom.

Action Steps

- Bring it into the light today with a trusted believer and ask for prayer and support.
- Remove access and triggers immediately: people, places, and patterns that feed relapse.
- Replace the habit with structure: sleep, exercise, prayer, Scripture, and daily routine.
- Speak 3 decrees daily for 30 days to rebuild self-control and renewal.
- Seek wise professional help if needed. Freedom is worth

accountability and support.

Accountability Move

Today, I will tell one trusted believer, "I need help staying sober. Please walk with me."

CLOSING PRAYER

Father, in Jesus' name, I repent for addiction, dependency, and every counterfeit comfort I've turned to. I renounce substance reliance, cravings, and every agreement with bondage. Holy Spirit, strengthen me, deliver me, and train me in sobriety, discipline, and clarity. I surrender my body, mind, and emotions to Jesus Christ as Lord. I declare that I will not be mastered by substances, and I will live free and whole. In the name of Jesus, amen.

CHAPTER 24

Break Free From Alcohol Dependence & Escapism

You don't need "a drink." You need freedom.

OPENING PRAYER

Father, in Jesus' name, I repent for using alcohol as comfort, escape, or control. I renounce dependence, addiction, and every pattern of numbing instead of healing. Holy Spirit, strengthen me, cleanse me, and lead me into sobriety, clarity, and freedom. Amen.

THE ISSUE

Alcohol dependence isn't always obvious. Sometimes it looks "normal" because it's socially accepted, but bondage doesn't become holy because it's common. Escapism is what happens when you use something to silence what God is trying to heal. And if you need alcohol to relax, cope, sleep, feel confident, or get through life, then alcohol is no longer a drink. It's a master.

WHY IT'S HAPPENING

- You're using alcohol to manage stress instead of surrendering it to God.
- You're numbing emotions instead of dealing with the root.
- You've built a habit that became a dependency.
- You've normalized "a drink" as your reward, relief, or escape.
- You're avoiding pain, pressure, or disappointment instead of confronting it.

WHERE IT CAME FROM

Alcohol dependence often begins as coping; especially when pressure builds and life feels heavy. It can be rooted in anxiety, loneliness, anger, exhaustion, rejection, or unresolved trauma.

The root is pain and escape, but the door stays open through repeated patterns, tolerance, and secrecy. And the lie underneath it sounds like this: "This is how I relax. This is how I survive." But escapism doesn't solve the pain. It just postpones healing.

BREAK FREE DECLARATION

I break agreement with alcohol dependence, escapism, and numbing in the name of Jesus Christ.
I reject the lie that I need alcohol to cope, relax, or function.
Jesus is Lord over my appetites, emotions, and habits.
I choose sobriety, self-control, and Spirit-empowered freedom.
I will not trade my calling for a coping mechanism.

SCRIPTURE-BACKED DECREES

1. I will not be mastered by alcohol. I declare that I refuse bondage, according to 1 Corinthians 6:12, "I will not be brought under the power of any."

2. God calls me to sobriety. I decree that I stay sober and watchful, according to 1 Peter 5:8, "Be sober and self-controlled. Be watchful."

3. Drunkenness is not God's will for my life. I declare that I reject intoxication, according to Ephesians 5:18, "Don't be drunken with wine… but be filled with the Spirit."

4. I choose the Holy Spirit over numbing. I decree that I will be filled with the Spirit, according to Ephesians 5:18, "but be filled with the Spirit."

5. Alcohol will not control my decisions. I declare that self-control is fruit of the Spirit, according to Galatians 5:22–23, "the fruit of the Spirit is… self-control."

6. I will not escape pain. I will surrender it. I decree that I cast my cares on God, according to 1 Peter 5:7, "casting all your worries on him."

7. God carries what I can't. I declare that God cares for me, according to 1 Peter 5:7, "because he cares for you."

8. Peace comes from prayer, not a bottle. I decree that I bring my needs to God, according to Philippians 4:6, "by prayer… let your requests be made known to God."

9. God's peace guards me from anxiety and craving. I declare that peace protects my mind, according to Philippians 4:7, "will guard your hearts and your thoughts."

10. My body belongs to God, not addiction. I decree that my body is His temple, according to 1 Corinthians 6:19, "your body is a temple of the Holy Spirit."

11. I will honor God with my body. I declare that I glorify God physically, according to 1 Corinthians 6:20, "glorify God in your body."

12. God provides a way out when temptation hits. I decree that God makes escape possible, according to 1 Corinthians 10:13, "will also make the way of escape."

13. I will resist the pull to escape. I declare that resisting the devil works, according to James 4:7, "Resist the devil, and he will flee from you."

14. Grace trains me to live sober. I decree that grace teaches discipline, according to Titus 2:11–12, "we should live soberly."

15. I will not return to what enslaves me. I declare that Christ sets me free, according to Galatians 5:1, "For freedom Christ has set us free."

16. Freedom requires firmness, not excuses. I decree that I stand firm, according to Galatians 5:1, "Stand firm therefore."

17. My mind will be renewed into new patterns. I declare that I am transformed, according to Romans 12:2, "be transformed by the renewing of your mind."

18. God strengthens me to break habits. I decree that God strengthens me, according to Isaiah 41:10, "I will strengthen you. Yes, I will help you."

19. I will walk in the light, not secrecy. I declare that walking in the light brings cleansing, according to 1 John 1:7, "if we walk in the

light… the blood of Jesus… cleanses us."

20. Confession brings cleansing and freedom. I decree that confession leads to cleansing, according to 1 John 1:9, "to cleanse us from all unrighteousness."

21. God heals what I have been trying to numb. I declare that God heals my wounds, according to Psalm 147:3, "He heals the brokenhearted."

22. God is close to me in weakness. I decree that the Lord is near, according to Psalm 34:18, "Yahweh is near to those who have a broken heart."

23. I will not waste my life on escapism. I declare that I redeem the time, according to Ephesians 5:16, "redeeming the time."

24. My identity is not "dependent." I decree that sin does not rule me, according to Romans 6:14, "For sin will not have dominion over you."

25. I will live clear, sober, and obedient. I declare that I walk as a child of light, according to Ephesians 5:8, "walk as children of light."

OBEDIENCE ACTIVATION

Confession

Jesus, I repent for alcohol dependence and escapism, and I surrender my coping patterns to You.

Action Steps

- Be honest today: admit whether alcohol is comfort, escape, or control.
- Cut access and routines that fuel dependence (stores, nights, certain people, stress triggers).
- Replace the habit with surrender: prayer, Scripture, exercise, sleep, and structure.
- Speak 3 decrees daily for 30 days to rebuild self-control and clarity.
- Bring it into the light with a trusted believer and ask for consistent

accountability.

Accountability Move

Today, I will tell one trusted believer, "I'm choosing freedom over alcohol. Help me stay sober."

CLOSING PRAYER

Father, in Jesus' name, I repent for dependence, escapism, and using alcohol as comfort instead of trusting You. I renounce addiction, numbing, and every pattern that keeps me bound. Holy Spirit, strengthen me, heal what's beneath the craving, and train me to live sober and free. I surrender my habits, emotions, and appetite to Jesus Christ as Lord. I declare that I don't need a drink. I need freedom, and freedom is mine in Christ. In the name of Jesus, amen.

CHAPTER 25

Break Free From Wrong Relationships & Soul Ties
Some connections are spiritual leeches.

OPENING PRAYER

Father, in Jesus' name, I repent for unhealthy relationships, ungodly connections, and attachments that weaken my obedience. I renounce compromise, emotional bondage, and every soul tie that keeps me stuck. Holy Spirit, give me discernment, courage, and clean separation where You require it. Amen.

THE ISSUE

Not every relationship is neutral. Some connections strengthen you. Others drain you, distract you, tempt you, and keep you spiritually numb. Wrong relationships don't just influence behavior. They influence hunger, identity, standards, and obedience. Because what you stay tied to will eventually shape what you carry

A soul tie is an unhealthy attachment that creates emotional and spiritual bondage. It can form through sexual sin, manipulation, control, addiction, toxic dependency, and prolonged compromise. And if you don't break it, you will keep feeling pulled toward what God is trying to remove.

WHY IT'S HAPPENING

- You fear being alone more than you fear being compromised.
- You're attached to someone who feeds your flesh, not your spirit.
- You confuse chemistry with covenant and connection with calling.
- You've ignored red flags because you're addicted to attention.
- You know the relationship is wrong, but you keep rationalizing it.

WHERE IT CAME FROM

Wrong relationships often begin when you're wounded, lonely, insecure, or hungry for affirmation. Sometimes you didn't choose connection out of wisdom. You chose it out of need. The root is often identity issues and fear of rejection, but the door stays open through compromise, emotional dependency, and sin. And the lie underneath it sounds like this: "I can keep this connection and still obey God." But partial surrender is still disobedience.

BREAK FREE DECLARATION

I break agreement with wrong relationships, ungodly attachments, and unhealthy soul ties in the name of Jesus Christ.
I reject the lie that compromise is love and bondage is connection.
Jesus is Lord over my heart, my relationships, and my obedience.
I choose holiness, discernment, and clean separation from anything that pulls me away from God.
I will not stay tied to what God is calling me to cut off.

SCRIPTURE-BACKED DECREES

1. God calls me to wisdom in relationships. I declare that walking with the wise makes me wise, according to Proverbs 13:20, "He who walks with wise men grows wise."

2. Wrong relationships corrupt my life. I decree that bad company corrupts good morals, according to 1 Corinthians 15:33, "Bad company corrupts good morals."

3. I will not partner with darkness. I declare that light has no fellowship with darkness, according to 2 Corinthians 6:14, "Don't be unequally yoked with unbelievers."

4. Unequal yokes are a trap. I decree that righteousness and lawlessness don't mix, according to 2 Corinthians 6:14, "For what fellowship have righteousness and iniquity?"

5. God commands separation from compromise. I declare that God calls me out of defilement, according to 2 Corinthians 6:17, "Therefore 'Come out from among them, and be separate,' says the Lord."

6. I will not touch what defiles my spirit. I decree that I remove what contaminates, according to 2 Corinthians 6:17, "Touch no unclean

thing."

7. God strengthens my boundaries. I declare that God gives me self-control, according to 2 Timothy 1:7, "power... love... and self-control."

8. I will guard my heart against unhealthy attachment. I decree that guarding my heart guards my life, according to Proverbs 4:23, "Keep your heart with all diligence."

9. I will not be led by lust or neediness. I declare that fleeing youthful lusts is wisdom, according to 2 Timothy 2:22, "Flee youthful lusts."

10. I will pursue relationships that honor God. I decree that I pursue righteousness and peace, according to 2 Timothy 2:22, "pursue righteousness, faith, love, and peace."

11. I will not return to people who keep me bound. I declare that God sets me free, according to Galatians 5:1, "For freedom Christ has set us free."

12. Freedom requires firm decisions. I decree that I stand firm, according to Galatians 5:1, "Stand firm therefore."

13. God will give me discernment. I declare that God gives wisdom when I ask, according to James 1:5, "let him ask of God... and it will be given."

14. My love will not be blind to truth. I decree that love must be sincere, according to Romans 12:9, "Let love be without hypocrisy."

15. I will hate what is evil and cling to what is good. I declare that I cling to what honors God, according to Romans 12:9, "Abhor that which is evil. Cling to that which is good."

16. I will not be manipulated by fear of rejection. I decree that God is my approval, according to Galatians 1:10, "If I were still trying to please men, I wouldn't be a servant of Christ."

17. God's peace guards me when I surrender relationships. I declare that peace guards my heart, according to Philippians 4:7, "will guard your hearts and your thoughts."

18. I will not make provision for compromise. I decree that I make no provision for flesh patterns, according to Romans 13:14, "make no provision for the flesh."

19. I choose holiness over attachment. I declare that God calls me to holiness, according to 1 Peter 1:15–16, "Be holy; for I am holy."

20. I will walk in the light, not secrecy. I decree that walking in the light brings cleansing, according to 1 John 1:7, "if we walk in the light… the blood of Jesus… cleanses us."

21. I will cut off what pulls me away from God. I declare that radical obedience is wisdom, according to Matthew 5:29, "If your right eye causes you to stumble… cast it from you."

22. I will not confuse "history" with covenant. I decree that old things pass away in Christ, according to 2 Corinthians 5:17, "the old things have passed away."

23. God has prepared a new path for me. I declare that God directs my steps, according to Proverbs 3:6, "he will make your paths straight."

24. I will be strengthened in my inner man. I decree that God strengthens me by His Spirit, according to Ephesians 3:16, "to be strengthened with power through his Spirit."

25. I will be connected to what produces life. I declare that remaining in Christ produces fruit, according to John 15:5, "He who remains in me… bears much fruit."

OBEDIENCE ACTIVATION

Confession

Jesus, I repent for wrong relationships and unhealthy attachments, and I choose obedience over connection.

Action Steps

- Name the relationship that keeps pulling you into compromise and be honest about its fruit.
- Set one clear boundary today (distance, no private communication,

no late-night access).

- Remove access points (social media, texting habits, meetups) that feed the soul tie.
- Speak 3 decrees daily for 14 days to retrain your heart toward clean separation.
- Replace the connection with healthy community and accountability in your local church.

Accountability Move

Today, I will tell one trusted believer, "I'm cutting off a wrong tie. Help me stay free and accountable."

CLOSING PRAYER

Father, in Jesus' name, I repent for ungodly connections, compromise, and attachments that weaken my obedience. I renounce wrong relationships, unhealthy soul ties, and every emotional bondage that keeps me stuck. Holy Spirit, give me discernment and courage to separate where You require it. I surrender my heart and relationships to Jesus Christ as Lord. I declare that every wrong tie breaks now, and I will walk in holiness and freedom. In the name of Jesus, amen.

CHAPTER 26

Break Free From Marriage Drift & Coldness

The enemy loves slow distance more than loud fights.

OPENING PRAYER

Father, in Jesus' name, I repent for neglect, emotional distance, and allowing my marriage to drift. I renounce hardness, selfishness, and every quiet compromise that has cooled love and connection. Holy Spirit, restore covenant strength, soften my heart, and teach me to love with intention again. Amen.

THE ISSUE

Marriage drift is when two people are still together... but not connected. It's coldness, routine, silent resentment, lack of pursuit, and emotional distance that grows slowly. Sometimes there aren't big fights. Just a slow fading of warmth, intimacy, teamwork, and honor. And that's exactly why it's dangerous: the enemy loves quiet distance because it's easier to ignore.

WHY IT'S HAPPENING

- You stopped pursuing and started coasting.
- You've let stress, work, and distractions take first place.
- You've allowed offense to pile up without dealing with it.
- You're giving your best energy to everything else, and leftovers to your spouse.
- You've neglected prayer, communication, and intentional love.

WHERE IT CAME FROM

Marriage drift often starts with fatigue and unaddressed disappointment. Small unresolved issues become quiet walls over time. The root is often selfishness and unhealed offense, but the door stays open through neglect, lack of communication, and emotional shutdown. And the lie underneath it sounds like this: "It's not that bad... we're fine." But "fine" is how marriages die slowly.

BREAK FREE DECLARATION

I break agreement with marriage drift, emotional coldness, and quiet
distance in the name of Jesus Christ.
I reject the lie that neglect is harmless or that connection will rebuild itself.
Jesus is Lord over my heart, my attitude, and my covenant.
I choose honor, pursuit, forgiveness, and intentional love.
I will fight for my marriage with obedience, humility, and truth.

SCRIPTURE-BACKED DECREES

1. My marriage is a covenant, not a convenience. I declare that God
   joins husband and wife, according to Matthew 19:6, "What
   therefore God has joined together, let no man separate."

2. I will not treat my spouse as disposable. I decree that covenant is
   serious, according to Malachi 2:14, "Yahweh has been witness
   between you and the wife of your youth… she is your companion,
   and the wife of your covenant."

3. God sees neglect and calls it out. I declare that God cares about how
   I treat my spouse, according to Malachi 2:15–16, "Take heed to
   your spirit, and let no one deal treacherously against the wife of his
   youth."

4. Love is not a mood. It's an action. I decree that I walk in love,
   according to Ephesians 5:2, "Walk in love, even as Christ also loved
   us."

5. I will love sacrificially, not selfishly. I declare that husbands are
   commanded to love like Christ, according to Ephesians 5:25,
   "Husbands, love your wives, even as Christ also loved the
   assembly."

6. My love will be patient and kind. I decree that love is patient,
   according to 1 Corinthians 13:4, "Love is patient and is kind."

7. I will not let resentment live in my home. I declare that bitterness
   must be removed, according to Ephesians 4:31, "Let all bitterness…
   be put away from you."

8. I will forgive quickly and completely. I decree that I forgive as

Christ forgave me, according to Colossians 3:13, "forgiving each other… even as Christ forgave you."

9. I will pursue peace, not emotional distance. I declare that I seek peace and pursue it, according to Psalm 34:14, "Seek peace, and pursue it."

10. My words will build, not wound. I decree that my speech gives grace, according to Ephesians 4:29, "that it may give grace to those who hear."

11. I will not neglect intimacy. I declare that marriage intimacy matters, according to 1 Corinthians 7:5, "Don't deprive one another… so that Satan doesn't tempt you."

12. I will stay alert against the enemy's schemes. I decree that I am watchful, according to 1 Peter 5:8, "Be sober and self-controlled. Be watchful."

13. Unity requires humility. I declare that I clothe myself in humility, according to 1 Peter 5:5, "clothe yourselves with humility."

14. I will be quick to listen and slow to react. I decree that I am slow to speak and slow to anger, according to James 1:19, "swift to hear, slow to speak, slow to anger."

15. Anger will not rule my home. I declare that I don't let the sun go down on wrath, according to Ephesians 4:26, "Don't let the sun go down on your wrath."

16. I will not give the devil a foothold in my marriage. I decree that I give no place to the devil, according to Ephesians 4:27, "Don't give place to the devil."

17. My spouse deserves honor. I declare that I honor my spouse with understanding, according to 1 Peter 3:7, "live with your wives according to knowledge… giving honor."

18. Prayer strengthens unity. I decree that I pray with humility, according to Philippians 4:6, "by prayer… let your requests be made known to God."

19. God restores what has been neglected. I declare that God restores what was lost, according to Joel 2:25, "I will restore to you the years

that the swarming locust has eaten."

20. I will not drift. I will pursue. I decree that I strengthen what remains, according to Revelation 3:2, "Wake up, and strengthen the things that remain."

21. God renews love when I repent and obey. I declare that God renews my heart, according to Psalm 51:10, "Create in me a clean heart, O God."

22. My home will be built on Christ, not coldness. I decree that Christ is my foundation, according to Joshua 24:15, "as for me and my house, we will serve Yahweh."

23. I will be faithful, not distracted. I declare that my eyes and heart stay guarded, according to Proverbs 4:23, "Keep your heart with all diligence."

24. God gives me strength to rebuild connection. I decree that God helps me, according to Isaiah 41:10, "Yes, I will help you."

OBEDIENCE ACTIVATION

Confession

Jesus, I repent for neglect and marriage drift, and I choose to pursue covenant love again.

Action Steps

- Initiate one hard conversation with humility instead of avoidance.
- Schedule intentional time this week to reconnect without distractions.
- Speak 3 decrees daily for 14 days over your marriage and your own heart.
- Apologize quickly for one area where you've been cold, defensive, or selfish.
- Pray with your spouse even if it feels awkward. Obedience rebuilds closeness.

Accountability Move

Today, I will tell one trusted believer, "Pray for my marriage. We're rebuilding connection and covenant strength."

CLOSING PRAYER

Father, in Jesus' name, I repent for distance, coldness, and neglect in my marriage. I renounce selfishness, offense, and every quiet compromise that has weakened connection. Holy Spirit, soften my heart, restore intimacy, and strengthen our covenant in Christ. I surrender my pride, my words, and my habits to Jesus Christ as Lord. I declare that marriage drift ends now, and covenant love will be rebuilt with obedience and honor. In the name of Jesus, amen.

CHAPTER 27

Break Free From Demonic Oppression & Torment
Some battles aren't emotional. They're spiritual.

OPENING PRAYER

Father, in Jesus' name, I repent for every door I've opened to darkness through sin, compromise, and agreement with lies. I renounce torment, oppression, and every spiritual attack assigned against my mind, peace, and purpose. Holy Spirit, fill me, strengthen me, and lead me into freedom through the authority of Jesus Christ. Amen.

THE ISSUE

Not every battle is psychological. Not every struggle is just trauma, stress, or personality. Some battles are spiritual resistance. Tormenting thoughts, heaviness, fear, condemnation, confusion, and cycles that won't break no matter how much you "try harder." Demonic oppression is when the enemy harasses, presses, and torments a believer's life from the outside. Through lies, pressure, and persistent attacks

This does not mean you're possessed. But it does mean you're under attack. And if you treat a spiritual battle like it's only emotional, you will stay stuck fighting with the wrong weapons.

WHY IT'S HAPPENING

- You've tolerated sin and called it small.
- You've made agreements with lies ("I'll always be this way," "God won't help," "I'm too far gone").
- You've stayed isolated instead of walking in the light.
- You've ignored prayer and spiritual discipline, leaving your life unguarded.
- You've been wounded, and the enemy has tried to build a nest in that pain.

WHERE IT CAME FROM

Spiritual torment often gains access through open doors: ongoing sin, unforgiveness, occult involvement (past or present), sexual immorality, substance reliance, bitterness, or habitual agreement with condemnation. Sometimes oppression intensifies during seasons of obedience because the enemy resists momentum.

The root is always the same: the enemy wants me bound, distracted, and weakened. And the lie underneath it sounds like this: "This is just who you are, and it will never change." But torment is not your identity. It's an attack.

BREAK FREE DECLARATION

I break agreement with demonic oppression, torment, and every attack against my mind and peace in the name of Jesus Christ.
I reject every lie, every fear, and every spiritual assignment that is not from God.
Jesus Christ is Lord, and His blood speaks better things over my life.
I submit to God, resist the devil, and stand in authority through Christ.
I will not live harassed, terrified, or bound. Freedom is mine in Jesus' name.

SCRIPTURE-BACKED DECREES

1. Jesus has given me authority over darkness. I declare that Christ gives me authority, according to Luke 10:19, "I give you authority to tread on serpents and scorpions, and over all the power of the enemy."

2. The enemy does not have power over me. I decree that all the enemy's power is under Christ's authority, according to Luke 10:19, "over all the power of the enemy."

3. I resist the devil and he must flee. I declare that resistance works, according to James 4:7, "Resist the devil, and he will flee from you."

4. My first weapon is submission to God. I decree that I submit to God fully, according to James 4:7, "Be subject therefore to God."

5. God has not given me fear. I declare that fear is not from God, according to 2 Timothy 1:7, "God didn't give us a spirit of fear, but

of power."

6. The Holy Spirit gives me a sound mind. I decree that God gives self-control, according to 2 Timothy 1:7, "love, and self-control."

7. I am protected by the armor of God. I declare that I put on God's armor, according to Ephesians 6:11, "Put on the whole armor of God."

8. This battle is spiritual, so I fight spiritually. I decree that my warfare is not fleshly, according to Ephesians 6:12, "our struggle is not against flesh and blood."

9. I tear down demonic lies and strongholds. I declare that strongholds can be demolished, according to 2 Corinthians 10:4, "mighty before God to the throwing down of strongholds."

10. Every thought must submit to Jesus. I decree that I take thoughts captive, according to 2 Corinthians 10:5, "bringing every thought into captivity to the obedience of Christ."

11. God is my refuge when oppression hits. I declare that the Lord is my refuge, according to Psalm 91:2, "He is my refuge and my fortress; my God, in whom I trust."

12. The Lord delivers me from fear. I decree that God delivers me when I seek Him, according to Psalm 34:4, "Yahweh heard me, and delivered me from all my fears."

13. I do not belong to darkness anymore. I declare that Jesus delivered me from darkness, according to Colossians 1:13, "who delivered us out of the power of darkness."

14. I belong to the kingdom of Christ. I decree that I have been transferred into His kingdom, according to Colossians 1:13, "translated us into the Kingdom of the Son of his love."

15. The blood of Jesus gives me victory. I declare that I overcome by the blood, according to Revelation 12:11, "They overcame him because of the Lamb's blood."

16. God's Word is my weapon. I decree that the Word is the sword of the Spirit, according to Ephesians 6:17, "the sword of the Spirit, which is the word of God."

17. Prayer keeps me spiritually alert. I declare that I pray at all times, according to Ephesians 6:18, "praying at all times in the Spirit."

18. I will not give the devil access. I decree that I give no place to the devil, according to Ephesians 4:27, "Don't give place to the devil."

19. My mind is guarded by God's peace. I declare that God's peace guards me, according to Philippians 4:7, "will guard your hearts and your thoughts."

20. The Holy Spirit fills me with power. I decree that I receive power, according to Acts 1:8, "you will receive power when the Holy Spirit has come upon you."

21. Jesus names and exposes the enemy's goal. I declare that the thief comes to steal, kill, and destroy, according to John 10:10, "The thief only comes to steal, kill, and destroy."

22. Jesus came to give me life, not torment. I decree that Jesus gives abundant life, according to John 10:10, "I came that they may have life, and may have it abundantly."

23. I overcome through God's presence. I declare that God is with me, according to Isaiah 41:10, "Don't be afraid… I will help you."

24. Deliverance is part of Christ's ministry. I decree that Jesus frees the oppressed, according to Luke 4:18, "He has sent me to heal the brokenhearted… to set at liberty those who are bruised."

25. Torment is not my portion. Freedom is. I declare that where the Spirit of the Lord is, there is liberty, according to 2 Corinthians 3:17, "where the Spirit of the Lord is, there is liberty."

OBEDIENCE ACTIVATION

Confession

Jesus, I submit to You, and I renounce every spirit of torment, fear, and oppression in Your name.

Action Steps

- Close doors immediately: repent of known sin, unforgiveness, and compromise.
- Speak truth out loud when tormenting thoughts hit. Don't stay silent.
- Pray daily with authority: submit to God, resist the devil, and stand firm.
- Speak 3 decrees daily for 14 days to retrain your mind and strengthen your spirit.
- Get accountability and prayer support in community. Don't fight alone.

Accountability Move

Today, I will tell one trusted believer, "I'm under spiritual attack. Pray with me and help me stand."

CLOSING PRAYER

Father, in Jesus' name, I repent for every door opened to darkness through sin, compromise, and agreement with lies. I renounce torment, oppression, fear, and every spiritual assignment against my mind and peace. I submit to God, resist the devil, and stand in the authority of Jesus Christ. Holy Spirit, fill me with power, guard my mind, and lead me in victory. I declare that torment breaks now, and freedom is mine through the blood and name of Jesus. In the name of Jesus, amen.

CHAPTER 28

Break Free From Anger & Rage

Unsubmitted anger becomes a doorway for destruction.

OPENING PRAYER

Father, in Jesus' name, I repent for anger, rage, and the damage my reactions have caused. I renounce bitterness, violence in my spirit, and every agreement with pride and control. Holy Spirit, soften my heart, govern my emotions, and teach me self-control. Amen.

THE ISSUE

Anger is not always sin, but rage usually is. Anger becomes a stronghold when it controls you, speaks through you, and punishes people around you. Rage turns your home into a battlefield, your words into weapons, and your relationships into casualties. And if you don't submit your anger to God, it becomes a doorway the enemy uses to destroy what you're called to protect.

WHY IT'S HAPPENING

- You've been carrying unprocessed pain and calling it "stress."
- You feel disrespected or powerless, so you react to regain control.
- You've normalized yelling, sarcasm, and intimidation as "just how I am."
- You're quick to speak and slow to listen.
- You're letting offense pile up instead of dealing with it in truth.

WHERE IT CAME FROM

Anger often grows from woundedness, injustice, fear, shame, and unmet expectations. Sometimes rage is learned behavior. What you saw modeled becomes what you repeat.

The root is often pride and pain, but the door stays open through unforgiveness, harsh speech, and a refusal to humble yourself. And the lie underneath it sounds like this: "If I don't explode, I won't be heard." But rage doesn't produce respect. It produces destruction.

BREAK FREE DECLARATION

I break agreement with anger, rage, and destructive reactions in the name of Jesus Christ.
I reject the lie that rage protects me or proves strength.
Jesus is Lord over my emotions, my words, and my responses.
I choose self-control, humility, and peace.
I will not let anger dominate my life or destroy what God gave me.

SCRIPTURE-BACKED DECREES

1. I will be slow to anger. I declare that God commands restraint, according to James 1:19, "Let every man be swift to hear, slow to speak, and slow to anger."

2. My anger will not control my mouth. I decree that I become slow to speak, according to James 1:19, "slow to speak."

3. Unsubmitted anger does not produce righteousness. I declare that rage doesn't please God, according to James 1:20, "For the anger of man doesn't produce the righteousness of God."

4. I will not give the devil access through anger. I decree that I give no place to the devil, according to Ephesians 4:26–27, "Be angry, and don't sin... Don't give place to the devil."

5. I will deal with anger quickly. I declare that I don't let the sun go down on my wrath, according to Ephesians 4:26, "Don't let the sun go down on your wrath."

6. My speech will not be corrupt or violent. I decree that corrupt speech stops, according to Ephesians 4:29, "Let no corrupt speech proceed out of your mouth."

7. My words will build, not destroy. I declare that my words give grace, according to Ephesians 4:29, "that it may give grace to those who hear."

8. Bitterness will not live in me. I decree that bitterness must be

removed, according to Ephesians 4:31, "Let all bitterness, wrath, anger… be put away from you."

9. I will forgive instead of punish. I declare that I forgive as Christ forgave me, according to Ephesians 4:32, "forgiving each other, even as God also in Christ forgave you."

10. Self-control is a fruit of the Spirit. I decree that the Spirit produces self-control, according to Galatians 5:22–23, "the fruit of the Spirit is… self-control."

11. I will not return evil for evil. I declare that I choose blessing, according to 1 Peter 3:9, "not paying back evil for evil… but… blessing."

12. Harsh words escalate conflict. I decree that I use gentle answers, according to Proverbs 15:1, "A gentle answer turns away wrath."

13. I will speak with wisdom, not heat. I declare that a gentle tongue breaks bones, according to Proverbs 25:15, "A soft tongue breaks the bone."

14. I will not live controlled by pride. I decree that pride brings destruction, according to Proverbs 16:18, "Pride goes before destruction."

15. I will humble myself under God's hand. I declare that humility brings grace, according to James 4:6, "God resists the proud, but gives grace to the humble."

16. God gives me a sound mind under pressure. I decree that God gives self-control, according to 2 Timothy 1:7, "power, love, and self-control."

17. Peace is a pursuit, not an accident. I declare that I seek peace, according to Psalm 34:14, "Seek peace, and pursue it."

18. My heart will be guarded so my anger stays submitted. I decree that I guard my heart, according to Proverbs 4:23, "Keep your heart with all diligence."

19. I refuse to be easily provoked. I declare that love is not easily provoked, according to 1 Corinthians 13:5, "Love… is not provoked."

20. I will not be ruled by resentment. I decree that I let go of offense, according to Colossians 3:13, "forgiving each other."

21. God heals what anger has been covering. I declare that God heals the brokenhearted, according to Psalm 147:3, "He heals the brokenhearted."

22. Jesus gives me peace where rage used to live. I decree that Christ's peace rules me, according to John 14:27, "Peace I leave with you. My peace I give to you."

23. I will return to obedience, not outbursts. I declare that I am a doer of the Word, according to James 1:22, "be doers of the word."

24. My life will be marked by gentleness. I decree that gentleness is from the Spirit, according to Galatians 5:22–23, "the fruit of the Spirit is… gentleness."

OBEDIENCE ACTIVATION

Confession

Jesus, I repent for anger and rage, and I surrender my reactions and emotions to You.

Action Steps

- Apologize to one person you've hurt with anger and take responsibility fully.
- Pause before reacting: breathe, pray, and choose self-control in the moment.
- Remove triggers that consistently escalate you (late nights, hunger, alcohol, isolation).
- Speak 3 decrees daily for 14 days to retrain your spirit toward peace.
- Deal with offense quickly. Forgive fast so rage doesn't build.

Accountability Move

Today, I will tell one trusted believer, "I'm breaking rage. Ask me if I'm staying submitted this week."

CLOSING PRAYER

Father, in Jesus' name, I repent for anger, rage, and destructive reactions. I renounce bitterness, offense, pride, and every doorway I've opened through unsubmitted emotions. Holy Spirit, govern my heart, train my mouth, and strengthen my self-control. I surrender my reactions to Jesus Christ as Lord. I declare that rage ends here, peace will rule my spirit, and my life will build and not destroy. In the name of Jesus, amen.

CHAPTER 29

Break Free From Financial Bondage & A Lack Mindset
Money doesn't rule you, and lack doesn't define you.

OPENING PRAYER

Father, in Jesus' name, I repent for fear, anxiety, and a lack mindset that has ruled my decisions. I renounce financial bondage, panic spending, and trusting money more than I trust You. Holy Spirit, renew my mind, teach me stewardship, and lead me into peace and provision. Amen.

THE ISSUE

Financial bondage isn't just about how much you have. It's about what money has in you. A lack mindset is the belief that you will never have enough. Enough time, enough resources, enough opportunity, enough stability.

It makes you anxious, controlling, stingy, impulsive, and reactive. And if you don't confront it, money becomes a master and fear becomes the advisor for every decision you make. God is not calling you to greed. But He is also not calling you to live enslaved to fear.

WHY IT'S HAPPENING

- You've been shaped by financial trauma and instability.
- You've lived in survival mode so long that peace feels unfamiliar.
- You're spending emotionally instead of stewarding intentionally.
- You're afraid of the future, so you panic in the present.
- You've believed "provision" is your job and not God's promise.

WHERE IT CAME FROM

A lack mindset often comes from real hardship: debt, poverty, job loss, inconsistent income, or family patterns that trained you to expect shortage. It can also grow in comparison, where you constantly feel behind.

The root is fear and insecurity, but the door stays open through anxiety, greed, impulsive spending, and refusing to trust God. And the lie underneath it sounds like this: "If I don't hoard, panic, or control money, I won't be safe." But money is a tool. God is your source.

BREAK FREE DECLARATION

I break agreement with financial bondage, lack mindset, and money-driven fear in the name of Jesus Christ.
I reject the lie that lack defines me or that money is my security.
Jesus is Lord over my finances, my decisions, and my future.
I choose stewardship, contentment, generosity, and trust in God's provision.
Money will not rule me, and lack will not name me.

SCRIPTURE-BACKED DECREES

1. God is my provider, not my paycheck. I declare that Yahweh is my shepherd and I shall not lack, according to Psalm 23:1, "Yahweh is my shepherd: I shall lack nothing."

2. Lack does not define my life. I decree that God supplies what I need, according to Philippians 4:19, "My God will supply every need of yours."

3. I refuse anxiety about provision. I declare that I do not worry about my life, according to Matthew 6:25, "Therefore I tell you, don't be anxious for your life."

4. God knows what I need before I ask. I decree that the Father knows my needs, according to Matthew 6:32, "your heavenly Father knows that you need all these things."

5. I seek God first, not money first. I declare that God's Kingdom is my priority, according to Matthew 6:33, "seek first God's Kingdom... and all these things will be given to you."

6. I will not serve money as a master. I decree that I serve God alone, according to Matthew 6:24, "You can't serve God and Mammon."

7. Contentment is strength, not poverty thinking. I declare that godliness with contentment is great gain, according to 1 Timothy 6:6, "godliness with contentment is great gain."

8. I will not love money. I decree that love of money is a trap, according to 1 Timothy 6:10, "For the love of money is a root of all kinds of evil."

9. My heart will stay free from greed. I declare that my life does not consist in possessions, according to Luke 12:15, "a man's life doesn't consist of the abundance of the things which he possesses."

10. God gives me wisdom to steward well. I decree that God gives wisdom generously, according to James 1:5, "let him ask of God… and it will be given."

11. I will work diligently with integrity. I declare that diligent hands rule, according to Proverbs 12:24, "The hands of the diligent ones shall rule."

12. I will not be trapped by debt. I decree that the borrower becomes servant to the lender, according to Proverbs 22:7, "The borrower is servant to the lender."

13. I choose generosity over fear. I declare that God loves a cheerful giver, according to 2 Corinthians 9:7, "God loves a cheerful giver."

14. God multiplies seed for obedience. I decree that God supplies and increases, according to 2 Corinthians 9:10, "He who supplies seed… will supply and multiply your seed."

15. I will honor God with my resources. I declare that I honor Yahweh with my wealth, according to Proverbs 3:9, "Honor Yahweh with your substance."

16. I refuse the spirit of poverty thinking. I decree that God gives power to get wealth, according to Deuteronomy 8:18, "he gives you power to get wealth."

17. God meets me in seasons of need. I declare that I have learned contentment, according to Philippians 4:12, "I have learned… to be content."

18. Christ strengthens me to be steady. I decree that I can do all things through Christ, according to Philippians 4:13, "I can do all things through Christ, who strengthens me."

19. I will not fear the future. I declare that God is with me, according to

Isaiah 41:10, "Don't be afraid… I will help you."

20. I will be faithful in small stewardship. I decree that faithfulness in little matters, according to Luke 16:10, "He who is faithful in a very little is faithful also in much."

21. God's peace guards my mind from panic. I declare that peace guards my thoughts, according to Philippians 4:7, "will guard your hearts and your thoughts."

22. My trust is in the Lord, not uncertainty. I decree that God is my refuge, according to Psalm 46:1, "God is our refuge and strength."

23. God gives me strategies, not chaos. I declare that God leads my steps, according to Proverbs 3:6, "he will make your paths straight."

24. I will build with purpose, not pressure. I decree that God prepared good works for me, according to Ephesians 2:10, "created… for good works… that we should walk in them."

25. I will steward with obedience and live free. I declare that freedom is mine in Christ, according to Galatians 5:1, "For freedom Christ has set us free."

OBEDIENCE ACTIVATION

Confession

Jesus, I repent for fear and lack mindset, and I surrender my finances and future to You.

Action Steps

- Write down your real fears about money and bring them to God in prayer today.
- Create one simple stewardship plan (budget, debt payoff, giving plan) and commit for 30 days.
- Stop panic spending and replace it with prayer and wisdom before purchases.
- Speak 3 decrees daily for 14 days to retrain your mind from lack to trust.

- Practice generosity in a small, consistent way as an act of faith and obedience.

Accountability Move

Today, I will tell one trusted believer, "I'm breaking lack mindset. Ask me if I'm stewarding with peace."

CLOSING PRAYER

Father, in Jesus' name, I repent for fear, anxiety, and financial bondage that has controlled my decisions. I renounce lack mindset, panic, and trusting money more than I trust You. Holy Spirit, renew my thinking, give me wisdom, and train me in faithful stewardship. I surrender my finances and my future to Jesus Christ as Lord. I declare that money does not rule me, lack does not define me, and God will provide as I obey. In the name of Jesus, amen.

CHAPTER 30

Break Free From Purpose Confusion & Lack of Direction

You were not saved to spectate. You were saved to build.

OPENING PRAYER

Father, in Jesus' name, I repent for drifting, wasting time, and living without clear direction. I renounce confusion, passivity, and fear that keeps me stuck in indecision. Holy Spirit, align me, clarify my assignment, and give me courage to move in obedience. Amen.

THE ISSUE

Purpose confusion is not always a lack of information. Sometimes it's a lack of obedience. It looks like overthinking, indecision, endless planning, and spiritual delay. It looks like being busy, but not effective. It looks like consuming teaching, but never building anything with it

God did not save you to spectate. He saved you to follow Jesus, to mature, and to produce fruit. And if you stay directionless long enough, you start calling stagnation "waiting on God."

WHY IT'S HAPPENING

- You're waiting for a perfect plan instead of obeying what you already know.
- You're afraid to choose wrong, so you choose nothing.
- You're comparing your path to other people's calling.
- You're distracted and undisciplined with time and focus.
- You want clarity without commitment.

WHERE IT CAME FROM

Purpose confusion often grows from fear of failure, fear of responsibility, and fear of not being "enough." Sometimes it's rooted in low identity. Where you don't believe God can use you. Other times it's rooted in comfort addiction. Where you don't want the cost of obedience.

The root is insecurity and hesitation, but the door stays open through passivity, delay, and distraction. And the lie underneath it sounds like this: "God will use me later… when I'm ready." But the call of God is not waiting on readiness. It's waiting on surrender.

BREAK FREE DECLARATION

I break agreement with purpose confusion, passivity, and directionless living in the name of Jesus Christ.
I reject the lie that I was saved to sit, stall, or spectate.
Jesus is Lord over my life, my time, and my assignment.
I choose obedience, clarity, and forward movement.
I will build what God told me to build, one step at a time.

SCRIPTURE-BACKED DECREES

1. God prepared my purpose ahead of time. I declare that God created me for good works, according to Ephesians 2:10, "We are his workmanship… created… for good works… that we should walk in them."

2. I was not saved to be idle. I decree that I walk in God's works, according to Ephesians 2:10, "that we should walk in them."

3. God directs my steps when I acknowledge Him. I declare that He makes my path straight, according to Proverbs 3:6, "In all your ways acknowledge him, and he will make your paths straight."

4. I will not lean on my own understanding. I decree that I choose trust over overthinking, according to Proverbs 3:5, "don't lean on your own understanding."

5. God will give wisdom when I ask. I declare that God gives wisdom generously, according to James 1:5, "let him ask of God… and it will be given."

6. I will not stay double-minded. I decree that double-mindedness brings instability, according to James 1:8, "He is a double-minded man, unstable in all his ways."

7. Delayed obedience is still disobedience. I declare that knowing and not doing is sin, according to James 4:17, "to him it is sin."

8. I will redeem my time with purpose. I decree that I redeem the time, according to Ephesians 5:16, "redeeming the time because the days are evil."

9. I will not waste my life on distractions. I declare that I walk wisely, according to Ephesians 5:15, "See then that you walk circumspectly… as wise."

10. God is not the author of confusion. I decree that God brings peace and order, according to 1 Corinthians 14:33, "God is not a God of confusion, but of peace."

11. The Spirit leads me, not fear. I declare that I am led by the Spirit of God, according to Romans 8:14, "as many as are led by the Spirit of God."

12. My purpose is connected to fruit. I decree that I bear fruit by remaining in Christ, according to John 15:5, "He who remains in me… bears much fruit."

13. I will not bury what God gave me. I declare that faithfulness is required, according to Matthew 25:21, "Well done, good and faithful servant."

14. God strengthens me to take action. I decree that God helps me, according to Isaiah 41:10, "Yes, I will help you."

15. I have courage through the Spirit. I declare that God gives power, according to 2 Timothy 1:7, "power, love, and self-control."

16. I will be steadfast and consistent. I decree that I stay immovable and productive, according to 1 Corinthians 15:58, "always abounding in the Lord's work."

17. I will run my race with perseverance. I declare that I run with endurance, according to Hebrews 12:1, "let us run with perseverance the race that is set before us."

18. God gives me strength to finish well. I decree that God completes what He started, according to Philippians 1:6, "he who began a good work in you will complete it."

19. My identity is secure in Christ. I declare that I am a new creation, according to 2 Corinthians 5:17, "he is a new creation."

20. My mind will be renewed into clarity. I decree that I am transformed by renewing my mind, according to Romans 12:2, "be transformed by the renewing of your mind."

21. I will seek God's Kingdom first. I declare that God's priorities guide me, according to Matthew 6:33, "seek first God's Kingdom."

22. God speaks through His Word clearly. I decree that God's Word is a lamp to my feet, according to Psalm 119:105, "Your word is a lamp to my feet, and a light for my path."

23. I will not fear man's opinion. I declare that pleasing people is bondage, according to Galatians 1:10, "If I were still trying to please men, I wouldn't be a servant of Christ."

24. I will walk as a disciplined builder. I decree that I train myself in godliness, according to 1 Timothy 4:7, "train yourself in godliness."

25. I will build what God assigns me to build. I declare that I am faithful with what I have, according to Luke 16:10, "He who is faithful in a very little is faithful also in much."

OBEDIENCE ACTIVATION

Confession

Jesus, I repent for drifting and indecision, and I choose obedience over confusion.

Action Steps

- Write down the last clear instruction God gave you and obey it today.
- Choose one area to build this week (prayer life, marriage, discipline, serving, outreach) and take daily steps.
- Remove one distraction that is stealing momentum (scrolling, entertainment, late nights).
- Speak 3 decrees daily for 14 days to retrain your mind toward

obedience and clarity.
- Stop waiting to feel ready and start moving in the direction of what honors God.

Accountability Move

Today, I will tell one trusted believer, "I'm done drifting. Ask me what I'm building this week."

CLOSING PRAYER

Father, in Jesus' name, I repent for purpose confusion, delay, and directionless living. I renounce passivity, distraction, and fear that keeps me stuck in indecision. Holy Spirit, align my heart, clarify my assignment, and strengthen my courage to obey. I surrender my time, my plans, and my future to Jesus Christ as Lord. I declare that I was not saved to spectate. I was saved to build, and I will move forward in obedience. In the name of Jesus, amen.

CONCLUSION

Stay Free. Keep Building.

If you've made it this far, I want you to hear me clearly: **I'm proud of you.** Not because you finished a book, but because you refused to stay stuck.

Most believers avoid this kind of work. They avoid confronting the hidden places. They avoid naming the strongholds. They avoid dealing with the patterns. They avoid the obedience it takes to actually change. But you didn't. You showed up. You faced what needed to be faced. You chose truth over comfort. And that matters more than you realize.

Now listen. Freedom is real, but freedom also has to be protected.

Because the enemy doesn't only attack you when you're weak. Sometimes he attacks hardest right after you get momentum. He'll try to pull you back into old thinking, old habits, old environments, old conversations, and old versions of yourself. He'll whisper, "See? Nothing changed." He'll try to get you to measure your freedom by how you feel instead of what God has said.

Don't fall for it.

Freedom doesn't always feel like fireworks. Sometimes freedom looks like quiet consistency. It looks like saying no when nobody sees. It looks like praying when you don't feel like it. It looks like closing doors you used to leave cracked open. It looks like obeying quickly. It looks like forgiving again. It looks like walking away from what you used to excuse. It looks like discipline. It looks like maturity.

And that is victory.

You don't need to be perfect to stay free. But you do need to stay submitted.

Stay in the Word. Stay in prayer. Stay in the light. Stay connected to a healthy local church. Stay accountable. And when you fall, because at some point you will stumble somewhere, don't run back to hiding. Don't let shame reattach chains that Jesus already broke. Confess quickly. Repent quickly. Get back up quickly. The enemy can't keep you bound if you refuse to stay down.

And I want to remind you of something that matters deeply: **you were never called to only "stop doing bad things."** God didn't free you just so your life could be less messy. He freed you so it could be more purposeful.

You were set free to build.

To lead your family with strength.
To love with maturity.
To stand with courage.
To pray with authority.
To serve with consistency.
To disciple others.
To live with clarity.
To be a threat to darkness.

So don't just celebrate what God delivered you from. Commit to what He delivered you for.

If you need to, go back through these chapters again. Open to the ones that still hit hard. Speak the decrees again. Obey again. Strengthen what remains. Because freedom isn't something you visit once. It's something you learn to live in.

And above all, keep this locked in your heart:

You are not disqualified.
You are not too far gone.
You are not stuck forever.
You are not powerless.

Jesus is Lord. The Holy Spirit is active. Scripture is true. And obedience still works.

So walk it out. One day at a time. One decision at a time. One act of surrender at a time.

You were not saved to spectate.

It is now time to leave the sidelines and build the Kingdom.

More From Mitchell Beecher

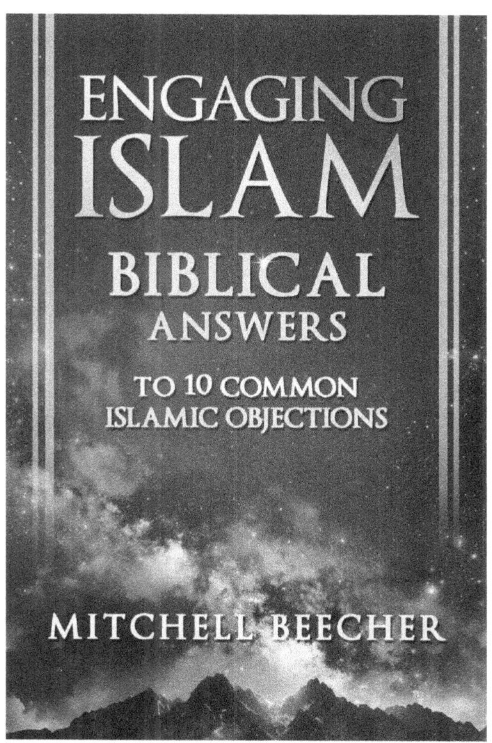

A clear, Scripture-anchored guide to help Christians confidently engage Muslims with truth, courage, and love.

If you've ever felt unprepared in conversations about Islam, this book equips you with straightforward answers to common objections and strengthens your confidence in Jesus Christ and the authority of Scripture.

Available on Amazon and at bekingdombuilders.com.

Keep Building With Be Kingdom Builders

If this book lit a fire in you, don't let it fade into another "good read." Freedom is protected through obedience, community, and consistency.

Learn more, get resources, and take your next step:
bekingdombuilders.com

New Life in Christ (Email Series)
A clear starting point for believers who want foundations, not fluff.

Courses + Tools
Biblical, practical resources designed to help you break patterns and build disciplined faith.

Community
A discipleship environment for believers who are serious about growth, accountability, and action.

Support the Mission

If Be Kingdom Builders has helped you, and you want to fuel the work, you can support the mission through donations. Your giving helps reach more believers, build more resources, and equip more builders.

Donate: bekingdombuilders.com/donate

Merch That Carries the Message

Wear the message. Start conversations. Put truth on display.
Explore BKB merchandise and support the ministry at the same time.

You were not saved to spectate.
You were saved to build.